Uncertainty and ambiguity are 2 things that every entrepreneur will face on a daily basis, and those things can, at times, cause entrepreneurs to feel paralyzed. Celia provides a masterclass in identifying the multiple types of fears that will be faced by entrepreneurs, but what's more, she provides clear tactics and action plans to overcome them. I believe this book should be standard reading for all entrepreneurs who are starting out, so they can be ready for the challenges ahead. As Celia states in her book "In the business world, monsters do exist" - best be prepared to battle them.

Paul Emond

Canadian Serial Entrepreneur with 30 years of
business experience, mostly in technology businesses

As an entrepreneur for more than 26 years, I related very quickly to many of the concepts Celia explores in her book. Following your dream is so much easier if you have tools and techniques to guide you step by step, particularly as you face obstacles, challenges and yes, fears. And Celia provides just that. This text is a truly valuable and practical resource for entrepreneurs at all stages of their journey, and I commend Celia for bringing it to life for us all to benefit from.

Lara Quentrall-Thomas MBA

Chairman, Regency Recruitment and Resources Limited,
Trinidad

This is an excellent book for new entrepreneurs. Celia clearly captures the internal and external fears that entrepreneurs will face as they set out on their adventure. Read it to prepare yourself for the challenges ahead and prepare yourself for success.

Tim Redpath
Executive Coach, Ottawa, Canada

This book has changed the way I think about starting a business. I have always thought about starting a business, but the thoughts have always been filled with trepidation. As the path ahead for me has been uncharted, my fears have always loomed like shadows in a dimly lit alley of uncertainty. Enter Celia Soonets' "The Wheel of 8 Fears of Entrpreneurs." With eloquence Soonets unravels the paradox of courage—the very essence that propels entrepreneurs forward. She invites us to shed the armor of vulnerability and embrace our fears as stepping stones toward growth. In the pages of this transformative book, I discovered that vulnerability doesn't have to be a weakness, it can be our greatest strength. Soonets dismantles the myth that successful entrepreneurs are impervious to fear, revealing that true courage lies in acknowledging our vulnerabilities. If you're an entrepreneur standing at the crossroads of fear and possibility, let Celia Soonets be your guide. Let the wisdom of The Wheel of 8 Fears of Entrepreneurs seep into your entrepreneurial spirit.

Janelle S. Ifill
Vice President, The Blue Financial Group, Barbados

THE WHEEL OF 8 FEARS OF ENTREPRENEURS

A Practical Guide to Recognize and Overcome the Fear of Entrepreneurship

CELIA SOONETS

Disclaimer:

The book *The Wheel of 8 Fears of Entrepreneurs* provides information and advice based on the author's experience and knowledge to provide guidance to readers. However, the author and the book's editors do not assume any responsibility for the consequences resulting from the application of the advice presented in this book, which is of a general nature and may not be suitable for all individual situations. The author and the editors are not liable for any loss, damage, or injury that may arise directly or indirectly because of the use or interpretation of the advice presented in this book. Readers assume full responsibility for their own conduct, decisions, and results obtained from the information provided in this book. The content of this book is not intended to replace or substitute for professional, medical, legal, or financial advice.

First edition, 2023

Content

ENTRY DOOR

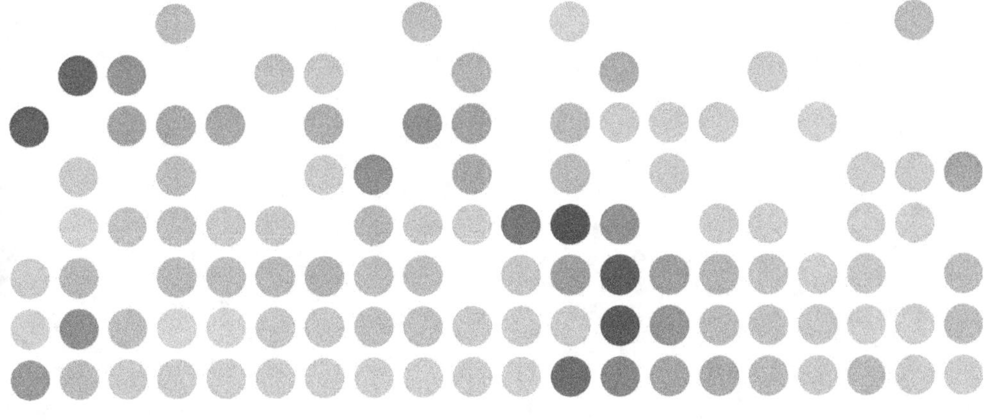

Let's start by accepting and highlighting three basic, concrete, and absolutely undeniable premises:

1. Everyone, without exception, has felt fear at some point in the past.

2. Everyone, without exception, continues to feel fear, often and on many occasions, in the present.

3. Everyone, without exception, will continue to feel fear in the future.

All human beings (in fact, all living beings) feel fear. Despite being such a universal, basic, and essential emotion, fear has an undeserved bad reputation. Historically and culturally, we have been taught that feeling fear is a sign of weakness. Through our socialization processes, we've been told that only cowards experience fear, that the brave never feel it. Consequently, we've learned to feel bad and even guilty when confronted with fear; we learn to hide it, to conceal it because we don't want to risk public scrutiny.

And this is a big mistake because, contrary to what many think and say, feeling fear is positive, prudent, and beneficial. Fear is absolutely necessary.

Repeat after me: Fear is absolutely necessary.

I don't want you to get the wrong idea that I believe we should all live in a constant state of fear or that it's healthy to live in fear. Fear is an emotion that naturally occurs in all of us at some point, but it can occur infrequently, and it can appear in very short, temporary episodes. In fact, that's usually how it is. When it settles in us with high intensity or as a permanent state, it becomes a condition that requires professional treatment.

The issue is not feeling fear. As I mentioned earlier, I insist now that feeling fear at times is beneficial and can even ensure survival since it can serve as an alert signal, preventing us from making wrong and risky decisions that could endanger us. **The problem starts when that fear paralyzes us and becomes an impediment to moving forward**. The setback arises when we don't understand that fear and, consequently, don't know how to confront it.

We must welcome fear. When it arrives, we need to identify it and, above all, understand it so we can tackle it, control it, master it, and overcome it if possible, or learn to coexist with it if it cannot be defeated.

Important Note:

The fear we will discuss in this book refers to those more temporary episodes, which are normal and can be controlled without professional help using certain strategies. If, after reading this book, you understand that the fears you experience are more permanent in nature, very intense, or very difficult to identify or control, I invite you to contact a specialized psychotherapist who can assist you properly. This book does not intend to replace the help of clinical psychology or psychiatry professionals who can provide specialized support if needed.

Let's return to the topic at hand: fear—specifically, the fear of entrepreneurship or the fear faced by entrepreneurs.

Entrepreneurs, as human beings, also experience fear. Many fears. Fears that are very specific and even intrinsic to the nature of entrepreneurship itself. We feel fear even before deciding to embark on entrepreneurship. We feel fear along the way. We may even fear when deciding to end or close our business. No entrepreneur can claim to have traversed the path of entrepreneurship without experiencing fear at some point in the journey.

As an entrepreneur, you may think you're alone in this journey. You may believe that only you can navigate these bewildering fears. Maybe when you assess other entrepreneurs, you get the impression that they don't have the same fears you face. Let me give you some news: even those entrepreneurs who appear more confident and whom you can't imagine being afraid have felt fear corrode them at some point in their entrepreneurship.

However, what often sets successful entrepreneurs apart from those who lag behind, is their ability to understand their fear, process it, overcome it, and ultimately use it as leverage, as a tool for growth and development of their business. Instead of remaining paralyzed and cowering due to fear, these entrepreneurs have managed to use it as a catapult, boost, and powerful motivation to reach their goals.

So, if you're interested in this book, if you've decided to open it, it's probably because you feel fear. And for that, I applaud you because you are part of that group of brave individuals who know, at least, to recognize it as an emotion. This alone indicates that you have the desire and intention to understand, control, and overcome it.

If you're an entrepreneur and you feel or have felt fear, this book is for you. It will help you not to feel alone. It will help you to understand that many entrepreneurs (I would even dare to say all entrepreneurs) have gone through the same tunnels or will face similar fears in the future.

There's a stereotype that portrays entrepreneurs as ambitious and arrogant, motivated solely by success and wealth, dedicating long hours to their business, sometimes above emotions and more "human" considerations. However, despite that stereotype, you and I both know that entrepreneurs are individuals who, while fighting for their ideas and working hard to achieve success, also have concerns, doubts, and dilemmas. Along the journey, we face an intense emotional world with uncertainties and ups and downs. And, as human beings, and due to the levels of risk and uncertainty involved in business activities, we often expose ourselves to situations that trigger some level of fear.

With this book, I want to offer you tools to help you understand your fears as an entrepreneur. I want to help you develop strategies to overcome them and advance in your business despite fear. I hope it proves useful to you and contributes positively to your success.

The book is structured into four parts. In Part I, we will discuss what fear is from the perspective of various disciplines that have studied it, and we will explore its manifestations. We will also understand why entrepreneurs feel fear. To conclude, I will present the conceptual model I have developed to understand the fear of entrepreneurs.

This conceptual model originated from many classifications I found in my research. I encountered theorists proposing as few as two or three basic fears, while others referred to more than twenty. I began with a simple exercise, which involved listing and organizing all the classifications of fears I found. I grouped them based on their similarities in meaning and manifestation. Through this exercise of theoretical analysis, I developed a model proposing eight basic fears entrepreneurs may face. Each has a different origin and manifestation and can be overcome with specific strategies. Fear initially arises when we confront change, which scares us because it is unknown. Four of these eight fears that make up my model are fears of "external" changes to the individual, or fears of things "happening." The other four I have defined as fears of experiencing "internal" changes in the person or, in other words, fears of "feeling" things.

After developing this theoretical model, I decided to validate it through research conducted between March and May 2023, involving 206 entrepreneurs from sixteen countries. The results of this study allowed me to refine my initial model, improve it, and quantify the relative importance of each of these eight fears.

In Part II, we will delve into the four fears related to external changes: the fear of economic losses, the fear of change in the rules of the game, the fear of competition, and the fear of operational problems. We will explain in detail what each one entails and how they manifest in the daily activities of entrepreneurs and analyze possible strategies to overcome them. At the end of each chapter, you will find a useful reference guide to help you identify, diagnose, manage, and overcome these fears.

In Part III, we will explore the four fears related to internal changes: the fear of feeling incapable, the fear of feeling like a failure, the fear of feeling uncomfortable, and the fear of being judged. As in Part II, we will explain what each one entails, how they manifest in the daily tasks of entrepreneurs, and, of course, analyze strategies to block them and not allow them to overwhelm us. Also, at the end of each chapter, you will find a reference guide to take actions that will help you put a name to these fears and leave them behind.

Part IV is your "toolbox." This book aims to be a useful instrument for you. It will not only allow you to learn about fears but also assist you with two critical matters:

1. Identifying which of all the fears we have discussed affect you the most at this moment in your entrepreneurship journey.

2. Preparing an action plan to overcome them.

Each entrepreneur may experience one or several of the fears considered in the conceptual framework. We do not necessarily face all of them, at least not at the same time. It's possible that, due to our personality or the nature of our entrepreneurship, we may never experience one, yet another may always weigh us down. It's essential to learn to identify them so we can confront and master them. In this final section, we will learn to recognize the different fears we may experience. In the toolbox, I offer a set of exercises that will allow you to identify your fears and create a plan to successfully combat them.

You can revisit these assessment exercises on future occasions or in relation to specific decisions you may need to make at another time. Fear is a living, dynamic entity that evolves with you. It can grow or diminish. It can change depending on the stage of entrepreneurship you're in. That's why the assessment you make when you reach this part of the book may not necessarily be the same as the one you would if you repeated the exercise next year, once the conditions of your business have changed.

The idea of this book is to be a practical guide. I hope reading it helps you create your plan (yes, yours) and make specific, concrete, and assertive decisions. Therefore, in the last chapter, I propose a methodology and a format to help you structure a strategic action plan that can contribute to minimizing your fears and, in turn, increase and enhance the chances of success in your entrepreneurship.

As I mentioned earlier, admitting that we harbor fear is embarrassing for many of us. So much so that we often not only refuse to reveal it to others to avoid judgment, but also avoid acknowledging it in the privacy of our own inner dialogue.

At this very moment, as you prepare to read this book, I invite you to discard any prejudices you have about fear. I urge you to set aside the misguided belief that feeling fear makes you fragile and weak. The first step in overcoming any complex or adverse situation is to accept and understand it. So, instead, welcome fear. Make it an ally in your journey as an entrepreneur. But, a word of caution: only invite it into your world as a partner who makes you more cautious, a personal system that gives you timely warning calls. Never use it as a leader who guides your steps. Don't give it more power than it already has.

Fear can be a poor advisor. Decisions we make when controlled and even hijacked by fear could be dangerous and lead us down the wrong paths. When we make decisions out of fear, we focus on minimizing the risks of possible negative consequences, not maximizing growth and success opportunities. That's what inspired me to write this book. To help you recognize your fears as an entrepreneur and learn to overcome them so that your decision-making comes from a foundation of opportunities rather than fears that can make you falter.

I hope you enjoy reading, and may these thoughts truly assist you in your practical decisions in the exciting and fascinating exercise of entrepreneurship.

PART I
FEAR

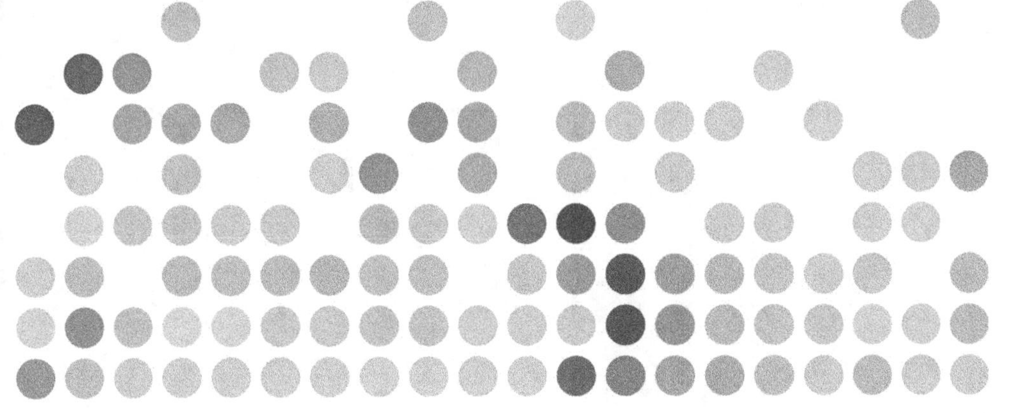

CHAPTER 1
WHAT IS FEAR?

*"Being scared is part of being alive.
Accept it. Walk through it."*

Robin Sharma

In this first chapter, we look into what fear truly is. To do that, let's start with the basics.

The Oxford English Dictionary (OED) defines fear as: *"The emotion of pain or uneasiness caused by the sense of impending danger, or by the prospect of some possible evil."*

From this formal definition, we can conclude that fear is an emotion that manifests as anguish and apprehension. In other words, it is an emotion of an unpleasant nature.

On the other hand, this definition indicates that fear is a wise response that occurs in the face of imminent danger. It is that unpleasant emotion we feel when we worry about the possibility of a dangerous, painful, or destructive event that is happening or could happen. In fact, it is an adaptive response of the body that prepares us to avoid or confront potential harm.

Fear is a prevention mechanism, an intelligent response of the body whose sense and purpose are to ensure survival. By alerting us to a potentially dangerous situation, it offers us the opportunity to react and seek safety or take action to confront an attack. If fear did not exist, we would be defenseless and exposed to many more dangers, with our physical integrity at unnecessary risk.

It is extremely important to understand that fear is an autonomous response of the body. Fear is not a voluntary reaction; it occurs automatically in response to a stimulus. This stimulus can be an external event (things that happen) or an internal event in our body (things we feel or thoughts anticipating that certain things might happen). So, the fear response not only occurs in response to observable and objective events but can also happen in response to events that are not real but are perceived as such or, even more so, imagined as possible.

The fact that it is an autonomous, non-voluntary response of the body means that we do not necessarily have control over when and under what circumstances it occurs. We cannot ask—let alone order—our body to feel fear, but we can, for example, ask our body to move our arm to reach for a coffee cup. Arm movement towards the coffee cup is voluntary; we can control when and how we want to do it. The fear reaction is beyond our will, and we cannot control when we want it to appear.

However, it is crucial to understand that it is possible to gain control over how we behave to confront and overcome fear once it is present. This is why the topic of this book is so relevant, as it can provide tools that enable control. If it were not possible to have some sort of restraint over our fears, the insight I offer would lack meaning and logic. Fear is controllable, and the response to fear can be educated.

Psychological Definition of Fear

Since fear is an emotion, and emotions are the subject of study in psychology, let's now explore the definition of fear from the perspective of this discipline.

According to J.P. Chaplin's Dictionary of Psychology, the psychological definition of fear is *"A strong emotional reaction involving feelings of unpleasantness, agitation, and a desire to flee or hide."*

From a psychological perspective, fear involves a subjective experience. As we will see in detail in the next chapter, this experience includes physiological, cognitive/emotional, and behavioral reactions. Psychology is particularly interested in deciphering fear's cognitive and emotional processes and understanding the social, environmental, and cultural stimuli that can trigger and modulate it. From a clinical standpoint, psychology also deals with understanding and addressing disorders related to fear when it is extreme, difficult to control, or affects the person's normal daily activities.

In our case, following this line of thought, with this book, we will focus on understanding the cognitive and emotional processes that impact an entrepreneur's performance. Likewise, we will try to comprehend the social, environmental, and cultural stimuli that affect the likelihood of successfully managing our business. Based on that, we will propose some strategies that allow us to re-educate our reactions to fear and redesign our behavior, enabling our attitude and actions to favor making the right decisions to capitalize on business opportunities.

Fear: That Basic Emotion

Fear is one of the basic, or primary, emotions. When we talk about primary emotions, we refer to those that are innate and universal to human beings and are expressed similarly in all cultures. In fact, they are not only innate and universal in humans but in all living beings.

Various authors have studied emotions. One of the most comprehensive and well-known theories on this topic is Robert Plutchik's "Wheel of Emotions" (1980). According to this author's model, there are eight basic emotions. These emotions can vary in intensity and can also combine, forming what he called advanced emotions.

According to Plutchik's framework, the eight primary, basic, or innate emotions, including fear, are as follows:

1. **Joy:** a sense of well-being, happiness, and satisfaction.

2. **Trust:** a firm belief that one can act without the danger of harm.

3. **Fear:** a feeling of apprehension or anxiety that arises in the face of a threat or danger.

4. **Surprise:** a sense of amazement, confusion, and astonishment at something unexpected.

5. **Sadness:** a feeling of sorrow, discouragement, and emotional pain.

6. **Disgust:** a sense of repulsion and rejection toward something unpleasant or disgusting.

7. **Anger:** a feeling of irritation, annoyance, and fury.

8. **Anticipation:** clear expectations about what will happen.

Pairs of these basic emotions combined give rise to more complex emotions, which Plutchik called advanced emotions. For example, fear combined with surprise generates awe, while fear combined with trust generates submission. Likewise, each of these emotions can occur with varying degrees of intensity, creating new emotions in turn. In the case of fear, when it is of low intensity, it is known as apprehension; when it is of high intensity, it is terror. In this way, we have a spectrum of complex emotions, all derived from fear. These basic and advanced emotions are a focal point for explaining the complex behavior of human beings.

Another interesting point of view about fear is the one provided by Dr. David R. Hawkins in his "Map of Consciousness", as outlined in his book Power vs. Force (2013). This map categorizes human emotions and states of consciousness on a scale from 1 to 1000, with 1000 being the highest level of enlightenment. Fear is one of the lower-level emotions on this scale. Typically falling within the range of 100 to 400 on Hawkins' scale, fear is linked to emotions such as anxiety, worry, and insecurity. At this level of consciousness, individuals often perceive the world as threatening, and there is a focus on self-preservation. According to Hawkins, emotions below the level of courage (200) can be debilitating and limiting, Fear being one of those lower-level emotions. It can lead to a narrow perspective, avoidance of challenges, and a resistance to change.

How Fear Is Generated in the Organism

The emotional response associated with fear is characterized by tension, anxiety, and/or apprehension, accompanied by physiological and behavioral activations that prepare us to either flee from danger or confront a situation we perceive as threatening our safety.

The emotion of fear originates in the brain. It is triggered when we receive information about stimuli we perceive as threatening.

This information reaches a part of the brain known as the amygdala. The amygdala is a small structure located in the brain, specifically in the temporal lobe, responsible for processing emotional information. The amygdala is a key structure in processing fear and considered the brain's emotional center. Together with other structures, such as the hypothalamus, thalamus, hippocampus, cingulate cortex, and insula, it forms what is known as the limbic system, which is responsible for regulating emotions and plays a crucial role in learning and memory.

It is not my intention to delve into the details of brain physiology. It is not the focus of this book, nor do I claim expertise in that area. However, I will try to explain in simple terms how it relates to fear:

When we are exposed to a potentially threatening stimulus, this information reaches the amygdala. If the amygdala detects danger, it triggers a fear response, which includes the release of stress hormones, an increase in heart rate, and preparation for a response behavior. This information then passes from the amygdala to other structures. For example, it activates the prefrontal cortex, responsible for decision-making and emotional regulation, and the hippocampus, which handles memory and contextualizing information. In this way, we learn that certain stimuli are dangerous, and our brain remembers this and how to reac.

And thus, a cycle of learning the response to fear is formed (Figure 1):

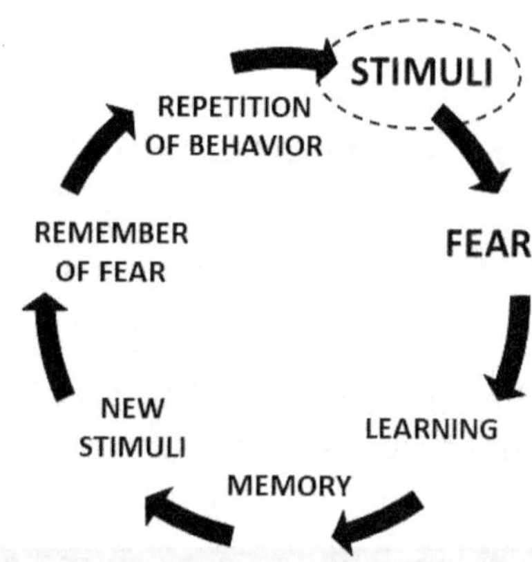

Figure 1 – Cycle of learning the response to fear

The Learning of Fear

As you can see, our brain processes information, learns that certain stimuli are dangerous, and stores them in memory. This constitutes an adaptive system for the organism's survival. Remember that fear's sole purpose is to ensure survival. We learn to experience fear in response to certain events and repeat this behavior each time they occur until, at some point, we change this learning with new learning, recording an alternative or different response to that stimulus in our memory.

Although fear is an autonomous response of the organism, the behavioral response we develop when exposed to fear is learned. This is excellent news. It means that no matter how deeply rooted a fear may be in our memory, with the proper techniques, we can "unlearn" or change the learned response to that stimulus, replacing it with an adaptive response that allows us to deal with that fear effectively. To achieve this, we must identify the various parts of this learning and memory cycle. We need to learn to identify what triggers this fear, how it manifests in us individually, and how we typically react so that we can consciously learn new strategies to face it or apply new ways of reacting.

And this situation described in the previous paragraph is what makes this book possible and potentially useful to you. The idea is to identify the stimuli that generate emotional fear responses in our entrepreneurial activities. We need to identify our current behavioral responses to them and learn alternative behavioral responses that allow us to react more adaptively. Are you starting to see how the possibility of a strategy to overcome your fears of entrepreneurship is taking shape?

In summary, fear is a mechanism of adaptation. It is part of our defense system. From a biological standpoint, it is a sophisticated and highly competent survival model for organisms. In neurological terms, it involves the activation of the amygdala in the temporal lobe. Psychologically, it is an affective and emotional state that generates distress. Socially, it involves cultural elements that sometimes lead us to learn to fear certain stimuli because we have been taught to do so. The truth is that we tend to repeat or reproduce specific cultural and social patterns from our environment. This leads us to question whether all fear is learned, or innate fears exist in organisms.

Fear is the body's natural and adaptive response to potentially dangerous situations. Some fears, such as the fear of loud noises or heights, may be innate and present from birth. These fears are part of the basic survival mechanisms that have developed throughout evolution to protect living beings. They are present not only in humans but also in animals. We are born with these fears "hardwired" to ensure our survival.

However, a significant portion of the fears we experience are learned. They are taught to us or developed in our psyche based on subjective experiences and cultural influences, as well as messages we receive from our family, friends, acquaintances, and the society in which we live. For example, the fear of spiders may have been learned by observing others react negatively to these animals or through some traumatic experience in our past.

It is important to note that while some fears may be innate, how we react to them and the intensity of our response can be influenced by external factors that are learned and acquired. Furthermore, fortunately, these innate fears can diminish or disappear over time and with exposure to the feared situations. In any case, it is possible to overcome learned fears through gradual and controlled exposure to these feared situations and with the help of a qualified mental health professional.

Types of Fear

In his book Practical Intelligence (2015), Karl Albrecht proposes a theory in which there are five primary fears. In fact, he constructs these five fears in a pyramid form, from the most basic to the most complex, in a manner similar to Abraham Maslow's well-known hierarchy of human needs (1943).

According to Albrecht's model, the five primary fears are defined as follows:

1. **Fear of Extinction:** This is the most fundamental fear, the base of the pyramid. It is the fear of ceasing to exist, of death.

2. **Fear of Mutilation:** This is the fear of losing a fundamental part of our body—the fear of losing a limb or an organ, of being disfigured.

3. **Fear of Loss of Autonomy:** This is the fear of losing the ability to be free.

4. **Fear of Abandonment:** This is the fear of being left alone, of losing our social relationships.

5. **Fear of Ego Death:** This is the fear of exposing our essence, our identity. This fear is at the top of the pyramid.

Albrecht suggests that the first three fears are automatic and related to survival. It would be unwise to try to eliminate them completely, as they are the primary defenders of our physical integrity. The fourth fear already begins to have elements of socialization and learning. The last fear, the fear of ego death, is primarily learned through socialization processes. According to Albrecht, this last fear is the one we have the greatest opportunity to shape.

Are the Fears Entrepreneurs Face Learned or Innate?

The fears that entrepreneurs face are generally learned fears. Our education and socialization processes, the cultural environment in which we develop, the country we live in, and the business sector in which we have embarked all contribute to our learning to feel certain fears in different forms and intensities. Our brains are inhabited by premonitions.

If we adhere to Karl Albrecht's classification, we could say that most of the fears entrepreneurs face likely fall into the last two levels of the pyramid: the fear of abandonment and, especially, the fear of ego death. Perhaps some might fit into level three, the fear of the loss of autonomy. In any case, they have a fundamentally learned component.

In many cases, these fears have developed to preserve our economic stability, protect our image, and help us avoid exposure to situations that may put us at a disadvantage with our clients, collaborators, and business in general. However, sometimes, these learned responses to face these fears, which lead us to try to preserve what we believe is order and stability, represent an anchor that prevents us from acting proactively to take advantage of new opportunities. When we decide out of fear, we limit the possibilities for the growth and development of our business.

Hence, it is of significant importance to learn to identify our fears and understand how and why we react to them so that we can generate new learnings. This book aims to change the fear-driven responses that lead to stagnation and wasted opportunities and teach you new responses to the stimuli that generate fear in you as an entrepreneur. It's about building new responses that, instead of representing an escape from opportunities, constitute behaviors that propel the wheel of your business development forward.

CHAPTER 2
HOW DOES FEAR MANIFEST ITSELF?

"The ghost is the outward and visible signs of an inward fear."

Ambrose Bierce

To comprehend and deal with fear, we must learn to detect and identify it. Only by knowing the signs that indicate the presence of fear will it be possible to realize that this is the emotion we are feeling and, consequently, activate an appropriate response.

Fear manifests itself in numerous ways. Some of these are quite evident and allow us to quickly and easily recognize that what we are indeed feeling is fear. Other signs are less obvious, and at times, it may be challenging to understand or accept that what we are experiencing is some form of fear.

Ah, fear has the bad habit of disguising itself so that we don't realize it is the one visiting us and trying to take up residence in our abode. Since fear has a bad reputation and we have been taught that feeling it is bad— and even cowardly—we sometimes prefer to paint it with the colors of other socially more acceptable emotions. We do not want to acknowledge that we are feeling fear. We believe it puts us in a position of weakness.

The main intention of this chapter is to expose fear and learn to recognize its manifestations and signs so that we can identify it and respond proportionally and appropriately.

Fear manifests in three different dimensions. It generates physiological responses, cognitive/emotional responses, and behavioral responses. All of them are designed to increase survival capacity. Many are not exclusive to this emotion and could be motivated by other circumstances. This is why it is sometimes difficult to identify and accept that fear is invading us. Let's examine these three dimensions of fear's manifestation in detail.

Physiological Manifestations of Fear

When we face an unknown stimulus that may be threatening, the body prepares to act. To do this, it reduces all non-essential functions and maximizes blood flow to major muscles. This can become evident in facial expression and, at the same time, produce a set of physiological responses, among which we can highlight:

- Increased heart rate
- Accelerated breathing or hyperventilation
- Cold sweating
- Tremors
- Palpitations
- Muscle tension
- Dilation of the pupils
- Dizziness
- Nausea
- Flatulence
- Diarrhea
- Increased metabolism
- Elevated blood pressure
- Increased adrenaline

Let's do a couple of exercises. First, think of a moment when you were aware that you truly felt fear in the past. It could be a moment when you were exposed to physical danger, in an accident, in front of a strange or dangerous animal, before an exam that you found extremely difficult, before entering an important presentation or work meeting, or when you were caught lying by your parents—any past situation in which you are aware that you felt fear. As you think of that moment nestled in your memory, try to remember if any of these physiological reactions occurred in your body. Since we are searching our memory archives for moments when we consciously acknowledge having felt fear, the memory and identification exercise is probably not very difficult. I bet that while you were reading this paragraph, some examples from your own history that produced some of these symptoms have already come to mind.

Now, let's do a different exercise. Think of moments when, for some reason, you felt some of these symptoms, but you did not understand or assume that you were feeling fear. Perhaps you associated them with passing discomfort, a virus, or a climate issue. Think if there were times in the past when you had these physiological reactions without being aware of the fear hidden behind them. This exercise is likely more challenging than the previous one. You may have never realized, for example, that you were feeling fear when you were sweating so much before going on the first date with someone you liked. The need to fit in with what is socially acceptable may have led you to attribute it to the fact that it was very hot in the place at that moment rather than to the fact that deep down, you were feeling fear of the uncertainty of meeting someone new you wanted to make a good impression on.

As you can see, not every time these physiological manifestations occur they are caused by fear. It is entirely true that we also sweat for many other reasons. Our breathing can accelerate due to emotions other than fear, and our heart rate can increase due to various circumstances. That's why it is sometimes difficult to identify fear. It finds it easy to disguise itself. We must be very attentive in order to identify it.

Of course, not every situation that triggers fear produces all these physical symptoms simultaneously, nor with similar intensity. The extent of symptoms you experience will depend on the specific circumstances and how strong you perceive the threat. However, all of these are possible manifestations that, when felt in response to a new or challenging situation perceived as threatening and whose outcome is unknown, should lead us to consider the possibility that such a situation has indeed caused us fear.

For example, this can happen to an explorer facing a wild animal, someone walking alone at night in a deserted place encountering a stranger who could harm him, a student taking an exam, or a professional working on an important project. Though we are talking about different situations, they can all trigger similar physical reactions when fear is unleashed.

Certainly, at some point in your life, you have faced various situations that have triggered some of these physiological manifestations. This would be a first indicator that the stimulus present at that time is something that, to some extent, caused you fear. I invite you to be especially attentive to these signs of physiological changes in your body from now on, and every time you experience any of these symptoms, take a moment to consider whether fear may have caused them.

I bet that in your journey as an entrepreneur, you have also faced circumstances that have raised your pulse, heart rate, or breathing or have caused tremors or palpitations. Perhaps meeting with a difficult client, the moment you realized (and accepted) that you could not fulfill a commitment, the moments before a presentation, or waiting for the approval of a loan. These are just a few examples of possible situations that generate fear in a business context and could cause some of these physiological manifestations.

Emotional and Cognitive Manifestations of Fear

In addition to physiological reactions, the fear response also generates cognitive and emotional manifestations. These responses are related to how our thinking receives, interprets, and processes the stimuli of fear and the emotions generated from them.

When perceiving a threatening stimulus and receiving the alarm signal, our mind tries to identify it to decide how to act. To do this, it relies on the information stored in memory. If the stimulus is identified as something that has caused harm in the past, or if it is a completely new and unknown threatening stimulus, an unpleasant emotion of anxiety or nervousness can be triggered, which can vary in degree or intensity from mild discomfort to a full-blown panic attack.

In essence, the cognitive response to fear is automatically triggered when attempting to discern whether the stimulus is novel or a situation we have encountered before.

If it is something new, the brain must use the available information to assess the level and context of danger and associated risk. If it perceives a prominent level of uncertainty or if there is certainty of possible harm, a strong emotional fear response can be generated. Conversely, if the evaluation of the stimulus and the analysis of available information indicate a possibility of having control over it, the emotional response may be more moderate.

If it is something known—that is, something we have been exposed to before—the brain will search the memory bank and retrieve available information on how we acted in the past in response to that threatening stimulus and how efficient and successful that behavior was in attempting to overcome the threat. The less control we were able to exert over our past behavior in the face of that threatening stimulus, the stronger the emotional fear response will be.

It's important to consider some differences between emotional and cognitive reactions. However, both are interconnected and play an important role in how we perceive and respond to the world. The emotional response refers to the emotions and feelings we experience, while the cognitive response focuses on mental processes related to knowledge and thinking. Thus, the cognitive reaction to fear is fundamentally an "evaluation" station in our mental process, which deals with identifying how familiar or new the threatening stimulus is, the likelihood that it will impact us negatively (cause harm), how much information or uncertainty we have, and how effective we have been when facing it. The greater the uncertainty and the greater the previous unpleasant experience, the stronger the emotional fear response will be. As we gather more information and have a more acute perception or history of the possibility of control, the emotional response will be less distressing.

Once this evaluation of the threatening stimulus is overcome, the emotional response occurs in line with the perception of the level of danger and the level of control achieved over it. This emotional response can manifest in many emotions, ranging from discomfort, mild nervousness, or restlessness to more severe ones, such as terror or a panic attack.

Let's look at some of these variations of emotional expressions that occur in response to fear. Some of these terms overlap; we often use them to describe similar states. Some of them are part of the same set of reactions, which, in addition to having similar definitions, can occur together.

1. **Excessive Worry:** People who experience fear often worry excessively about what might happen. They may have repetitive thoughts about the object or situation that scares them.

2. **Nervousness:** A transient state of nervous excitement that produces restlessness or a lack of tranquility. The person may feel anxious, restless, or uneasy about the situation that frightens them. This emotional response is possibly the mildest state of this type of emotion. It can make it difficult for us to concentrate.

3. **Stress:** A state of tension and emotional pressure. When we are stressed or under stress, we feel overwhelmed by the situation that intimidates us, and it becomes difficult for us to face it.

4. **Insecurity:** Fear can make us feel vulnerable and provoke a sense of insecurity. We can feel threatened or defenseless against

the unsettling situation without knowing what to do to protect ourselves.

5. **Anxiety:** Can manifest as worry, unease, or a persistent fear that seemingly has no end. The main characteristic of anxiety is that it is an anticipatory state. It plays tricks on us and makes us produce an anticipated response to what is perceived as potentially dangerous.

6. **Hopelessness:** The feeling that all possibility of control has been lost. It implies a pessimistic view of the possibilities of resolving the problem.

7. **Depression:** Prolonged or chronic fear can lead to an insidious sense of hopelessness, despair, and sadness in a person on a more permanent basis, resulting in depression.

8. **Panic Attacks:** In extreme cases, fear can trigger episodes of panic, with an elevated level of anxiety that can lead to severe physical symptoms such as excessive sweating, palpitations, shortness of breath, and a disturbance in balance. Excessive fear, even if unjustified, fuels more fear.

Some of these emotional responses to fear are mild and can be easily managed with appropriate strategies and techniques. Others, such as anxiety disorders, panic attacks, and depression, are considered more severe disorders that hinder the proper functioning of the body and require the assistance of specialized professionals. *As I have mentioned in previous chapters, this book does not aim to be a solution to these severe states of fear. If you believe that the fears you face in your personal life or your entrepreneurship fall into any category considered high-intensity, I invite you to seek help from a therapist who specializes in these types of disorders.*

Pilar Jericó, in her book NoMiedo (NoFear) (2006), proposes a classification of these emotional responses to fear based on two dimensions: intensity and duration. Considering her classification, this book aims to help you identify and control low-intensity fear responses, whether they are of short or long duration, related to your entrepreneurial activity. *If your case falls into a high-intensity category, I encourage you to seek a psychotherapist specializing in these disorders.*

Behavioral Manifestations of Fear

Let's talk about the behaviors that are generated as a response to the emotion of fear. A threatening stimulus that triggers fear can produce four possible basic reactions:

1. **Confrontation with the stimulus to fight against it and dominate it.** For example, let's say that if we encounter a robber who has surprised us on our way home, we decide to do something that eliminates the possibility of harm: we confront him, defend ourselves, and remove him from the environment where he can harm us. Confrontation can take other forms, such as alertness or vigilance, where we anticipate the possibility of the stimulus appearing and then stay prepared to act. In the example of the robber, if we know that it's an area where we are likely to be attacked, we come prepared with what's needed to subdue him and with our senses alert so that he doesn't catch us off guard. This could be considered preemptive confrontation. Another variant of confrontation is seeking help or support, where we confront the threatening stimulus but don't do it alone. In the example of the robber, we would ask for someone to come to our aid.

2. **Fleeing from the stimulus to get away from it and avoid harm.** In the same example, instead of confronting the robber, we decide to run away or move to a physical space where the robber can't reach us. We withdraw from his area of influence to be safe from the potential threat. A variation of fleeing is avoidance behavior. Once we learn that the stimulus causes us fear, we try to prevent it from taking us by surprise. To do that, we move away from the possibility of encountering that threatening stimulus. If we know that street muggers frequently attack in a particular area, we avoid that route.

3. **Freezing in front of the stimulus.** In this case, we become incapacitated to act. We do nothing. We simply become scared but immobile. In the example of the robber, we don't confront him, don't ask for help, and don't run away. We surrender, hoping that the situation won't escalate.

4. **Extreme compliance with the stimulus, or fawning.** This term describes the attitude or behavior of a person who shows excessive satisfaction or unquestioning acceptance of a situation or circumstance, even when it could be inappropriate or problematic. It can lead to ignoring the threat. In the case of the robber, we try to win his sympathy with compliments, seeking to please him, generate some empathy, and even mimic him to dissuade him from harming us.

All these behaviors are considered defensive. They are reactions activated in response to a threatening stimulus as a protective mechanism.

The response of confronting the fear-inducing stimulus, fleeing from it, or avoiding it depends on our brain's assessment of the likelihood of success in confronting it. If the probability of success is high, there is a behavior of confrontation. If the probability of success is low, we validate a behavior of escape. We must be overly cautious in this assessment because when our brain's evaluation is wrong, we expose ourselves to situations where we recklessly face dangers that we are not adequately prepared to control. It could also happen that we flee from situations that we could confront successfully using the tools and resources available.

The worst possible response to the fears entrepreneurs face is paralysis or inaction. I hope to help you accurately assess the threats your business faces so that you can develop the right strategies to confront them or the appropriate judgment to avoid them or distance yourself from them if your chances of success are low.

CHAPTER 3
WHY DO ENTREPRENEURS FEEL FEAR?

"As an entrepreneur, two things you'll experience every day are fear of the unknown and uncertainty. To run a successful business, you'll need to face these fears."

Darren Hardy

In the two previous chapters, we have made it clear that feeling fear, to some extent, is normal and even healthy. Feeling fear does not make you a coward or a weak person. Feeling fear means that you are a normal human being, with your alert systems functioning properly to keep you safe from dangers or risks. We have also established that fear is triggered by the unknown, preventing us from acting recklessly and grounding us in a reality check.

The thing is, when we are entrepreneurs, the unknown and uncertainty accompany us all the time. That's why fear arises. The fears of an entrepreneur are part of an alert system that compels us to stop and think because we are constantly dealing with changing environments, uncertain futures, and little certainty about the real consequences of the actions we can or should take.

Of course, there is always some level of uncertainty when we are employees. Still, in general, we tend to have more certainty because we have delegated a good part of the responsibility to higher levels of management. We know what is expected of us, we are secure about when and how much we will be paid, and we know the rules. However, the unknown is a big part of an entrepreneur's daily life. And that, whether we like it or not, generates fear. The perception that we have no control over the future is the leading cause of the appearance of entrepreneurial fears.

The problem is not fear. The real problem arises when we get stuck, and fear prevents us from deciding and moving forward once we have weighed the situation. Fear can lead us to rush, to make hasty decisions that will later seem absurd. And fear can sometimes lead us not to make or postpone decisions that could help us overcome obstacles.

All the decisions we make along our entrepreneurial journey, whether big or small, in moments of success or failure, involving personal or professional matters, carry a great deal of uncertainty.

Every decision we make implies a risk, even if it's small, because it may involve discarding an alternative decision that might have been more favorable. After all, on many occasions, every time we decide, we are deciding "not to do" or "not to choose" a lot of alternative options that were available.

Let's imagine that when we must make a decision about our entrepreneurship, we are standing in front of various doors. Every time we decide to open one of those doors, we are taking the risk of facing what's behind it, but, in addition, we are choosing not to open the other doors.

Unfortunately, not all doors lead to growth opportunities. There are doors we open because we rush into making decisions without thinking. And there are other doors we open out of fear. And doors we leave closed because they seem very heavy and difficult to open, even though they might lead us to a better path. And finally, there are doors that would be good options, but we don't even consider them because we don't have all the necessary information.

To increase the chances of opening the most convenient door, of making decisions that will benefit us, we need to gather as much information as possible about the elements that affect the decision. We must focus on anything that reduces uncertainty about what is on the other side of that door we want to cross. The more information we have, the greater the certainty about what might happen based on our decision.

But it's not enough to have information about the decision we want to make. We must also thoroughly evaluate the alternatives, those other doors we could open. In this way, we try to lower the levels of uncertainty and optimize the likelihood of choosing what is most advantageous.

The uncertainty of not knowing what is behind each door produces fear in us. If we had absolute certainty, there would be no room for the entrepreneur's fear because we could always count on the security that we have control over the consequences of our decisions. We would always know what to expect.

But that ideal scenario in which we know with certainty what is behind each door simply does not exist. So many times, we feel fear when considering which door to open. And then we face the possibility, undesirable and inconvenient, of deciding out of fear.

What Happens to Our Decisions as Entrepreneurs When We Feel Fear?

We have already established that when we feel fear, four possible behavioral responses generally occur: confrontation, flight, paralysis, or fawning. Neither confrontation nor flight is better than the other. The correctness of each depends on the probability of being successful in our response. As you probably suspect, the correctness of the response will depend on the information we have about which option (to flee or confront) is more likely to be successful.

The third possible behavioral response, paralysis, namely, doing nothing, can quickly lead to the failure of the business. Whoever doesn't even attempt to achieve something has already failed.

We know that fear is a necessary emotion. When we don't feel fear, we don't measure the consequences, we don't restrain ourselves, we don't analyze. We tend to be impulsive. And that can lead us to one failure after another. However, it is also a problem if we allow fear to dictate our decision-making. When we act under the persistent effect of fear, we focus our attention on a few stimuli. And if we focus on a few things, we don't objectively evaluate all the necessary information. We see the trees, not the forest. We don't use all the resources we have to reduce uncertainty. When fear subsides, there is muscle relaxation, heart rate drops, and breathing calms. That's when we should make decisions. Calmly. Decisions made from fear generate more anxiety, whereas decisions made from calm and growth generate tranquility.

When we make decisions based on fear, we risk making a decision that is not the most suitable for the situation or may have negative long-term consequences.

What Decisions are Promoted by Fear?

The following are possible decisions that occur when we decide out of fear. That is, decisions we make when we face a lot of uncertainty and are in a state of agitation:

1. **Escape decisions instead of decisions that bring us closer to the goal:** When we run away and prefer not to continue towards our goals for fear of failure.

2. **Procrastination of decisions:** When we know it's time to decide because not deciding on time is itself a wrong decision, but we are so afraid of opening the wrong door that we prefer the problems that come with non-decision (which we know) over the potential problems that could come from a wrong decision.

3. **Changing decisions:** When we make decisions and do not stick to them for fear of assuming the consequences that come with consistency and commitment to a course of action.

4. **Absurd sacrifices:** When we decide, with an unusual and perhaps unnecessary stoicism, to sacrifice things that could have been salvaged along the way without affecting the goal.

5. **Decisions that don't "feel" right:** When we make a decision that we don't really agree with. We've all been through this at some point. We decide on an option for several reasons, but deep down, we intuit—"feel"—that it's not the right decision.

6. **Emergencies that distract from the goal:** When pressured by an unforeseen circumstance, we decide without considering how much that decision takes us away from our focus.

7. **Decisions driven by the judgments of others:** When we decide based on what we think will be "better seen" or "approved" by others. Often, the best decisions are difficult and are not always understood by everyone involved or interested, at least in the short term. We should not allow the judgment of others to be a decisive factor, although it can be one to consider when evaluating alternatives and scenarios.

Deciding from Opportunity, Not Fear

As entrepreneurs, we must change our focus. Instead of deciding from fear, we can decide from opportunity.

Fear is undoubtedly an alert system. But it can be a poor advisor. We should allow fear to provide us with a warning on our path. However, once we acknowledge the service it has provided with its warning, we should set it aside and not allow it to manipulate our decisions. Fear can cloud our judgment. In some cases, fear can divert us from the best path, causing us to avoid important situations or decisions that could ultimately benefit us.

When we make decisions from fear, we focus on trying to circumvent a negative situation or one involving risks. Instead of seeking opportunities, we focus on minimizing risks and potential negative consequences. This can often lead to overly conservative decisions that hinder growth and progress.

On the contrary, when we make decisions from opportunity, we focus on taking advantage of a situation to gain a benefit or advantage. This may well involve taking risks and making daring decisions, but it can also offer great opportunities for growth and success.

Tolerance for Uncertainty and Ambiguity

When making decisions, there is always an element of uncertainty. Lack of information generates ignorance and confusion. False, unverified information also creates uncertainty. Excess information is confusing and certainly generates uncertainty. And uncertainty generates fear: fear of making mistakes, fear of losing, fear of looking bad.

Many of us have been raised to value a stable job more than entrepreneurship. We have been molded for security, for predictability. The ability to deal with ambiguity and uncertainty is not a skill often taught to us from a young age. And when we choose the path of entrepreneurship, that is an indispensable skill because we must live with ambiguity and uncertainty every tiny step of the way.

One of the origins of the entrepreneur's fears, then, is the ambiguity they face. In this sense, an essential skill for dealing with the fears of the entrepreneur and learning to overcome them is developing a tolerance for ambiguity and uncertainty.

Once again, let's turn to the basic definitions. The Oxford English Dictionary defines *"ambiguous"* as *"Having different possible meanings; open to more than one interpretation."*

When we talk about tolerance for ambiguity, we refer to the ability to successfully navigate uncertain, unpredictable, and unknown environments.

The concept of Tolerance for Ambiguity was first introduced as a psychological construct by Elsa Frenkel-Brunswik in 1949. According to Frenkel, tolerance for ambiguity describes the intensity of individuals' relationship with ambiguous stimuli or events, ranging from low tolerance (very intense reaction) to high tolerance (low-intensity reaction).

Subsequent studies (Budner, 1962) defined low tolerance for ambiguity as the tendency to perceive ambiguous situations as sources of threat, while high tolerance was defined as the tendency to perceive them as desirable situations.

In summary, lower tolerance indicates a greater rejection of ambiguous situations or stimuli and, therefore, a stronger negative reaction to them, while higher tolerance indicates less rejection and, therefore, a better disposition to accept them. Low levels of tolerance for ambiguity have been associated with higher levels of anxiety and stress, while high levels of tolerance for ambiguity are linked to greater openness to new experiences and better adaptability to change.

Tolerance for Ambiguity, Anxiety, and Stress

From these definitions, we can begin to understand how developing greater tolerance for ambiguity is positive for entrepreneurs because:

1. It reduces levels of anxiety and stress.

2. It promotes openness to adaptation and adjustment.

As a result, it puts us in a better position to accept ambiguity as part of opportunities for development and growth.

Developing greater tolerance for ambiguity involves learning to stay in control in the face of uncertainty despite the discomfort that not having answers to questions or not knowing where we are heading may cause. By nature, the human mind tends to seek balance. Any source of imbalance generates responses of dissatisfaction that can manifest as escape (to avoid the source of imbalance), paralysis (because we don't know how to react) or seeking to restore balance (action). The response that most promotes development is action, consciously seeking to learn from the imbalance and understanding it as an opportunity for new ways to restore the lost balance.

The leading cause of perceiving a situation or stimulus as ambiguous is inadequate information. It may be that the information we have is incomplete, vague, or possibly contradictory. The lack of precise information produces ambiguity in perception. When a situation is ambiguous, there is no clear relationship between possible courses of action and their corresponding consequences, so there is no certainty about optimizing the chances of success. Without sufficient information, we will not know how to act on it assertively. In this sense, the best way to deal with ambiguity is by seeking information to dispel uncertainties and thus clarify our vision, enabling us to act promptly, creatively, and openly.

Responsibility and Fear

Another crucial element that contributes to fueling entrepreneurs' fears is the need to assume responsibilities.

Entrepreneurs accept great responsibility when starting a business. When we embark on entrepreneurship, we shoulder the burden of being the ultimate decision-makers. There is no longer a boss to turn to, lean on, or blame for mistakes. Any decision that is made, even if it's made by our employees, ultimately falls to us.

This is particularly relevant when businesses are small because there is limited structure, and we must take on a multitude of tasks and face a wide range of decisions. But it's also relevant when businesses are larger because, even with teams in place, as the heads of the entire structure, we must take responsibility for our decisions or those of our employees.

Taking the reins generates fear and anxiety in the daily life of an entrepreneur because it forces us to accept that we may have failed, made a wrong decision, or are simply avoiding making a decision. We may fear being unable to handle all the tasks and decisions of managing a company. The responsibility of managing investors' or employees' money can be daunting. The possibility of not generating enough income to meet all financial commitments can be distressing. If mistakes are made that affect our customers due to offering deficient products or services, it is we who must face the consequences and take responsibility on behalf of our business.

This greater responsibility can be accompanied by greater fear. Responsibility puts us in a position where our actions and decisions can significantly impact others. This can create fear of making mistakes or not meeting expectations. Assuming responsibilities often exposes us to a greater emotional burden.

Locus of Control

From a young age, assuming responsibilities has always been difficult, mainly due to fear of consequences. When we are children, it is common to try to evade responsibilities by placing the cause of our actions outside of ourselves. We tend to blame our little sibling, the teacher, or even bad luck for things that happen to us, even when the "blame" is often ours.

I don't like the word "blame" because of its negative connotations. "Blame" implies admitting to something that is wrong and requires punishment. I prefer to use the term "responsibility." So, let's change the last sentence of the previous paragraph to: "When many times the responsibility is ours." The term "responsibility," unlike "blame," allows us to take control. Instead of punishment, we have an opportunity to correct and generate positive change.

"Taking responsibility for something" implies accepting the consequences of our actions. It means not attributing control to external entities and starting to accept our role in what happens to us. Taking responsibility is imperative for an entrepreneur's success.

Returning to the example of children, it is primarily the task of parents and educators to adequately convey the concept that we have control over most of the things that happen in our lives. It must be taught that we can begin to grow and develop to our full potential only when we stop pointing fingers at others. When this is not adequately conveyed to a child at an early age, there is a tendency to reproduce an attitude in which we learn to complain about what happens to us and place the responsibility for change on external entities. As adults, it will no longer be the little sibling or the teacher but the boss, coworkers, or the government. It will no longer be bad luck but what God wants for us or what destiny has in store for us.

This reflection leads us to a concept that has stuck with me and opened my eyes ever since I learned it many years ago when I was studying psychology. It's the concept of the "Locus of Control." The Locus of Control is a concept introduced by Julian Rotter in 1954 within the framework of Personality Psychology. It refers to the extent to which people believe they have control over what happens in their lives. The Locus of Control is presented as a continuum ranging from an External Locus of Control to an Internal Locus of Control.

Individuals with an External Locus of Control are inclined to attribute the control of events in their lives to external factors or other people. They absolve themselves of responsibility. This is where statements blaming government policies, other people, or destiny arise.

On the other hand, people with a strong Internal Locus of Control understand their position, assume responsibility for the events that affect them, and realize that the things that happen to them are often caused by their own decisions.

The Locus of Control is considered a personality trait; therefore, it is relatively stable over time. However, this does not mean it is immutable and cannot be re-educated and developed. It is a personality trait, but it determines the attitude with which we face life, both personally and professionally. Therefore, it is susceptible to training and modification.

An Internal Locus of Control is indispensable for entrepreneurs. Why is this topic so important for our perspective as entrepreneurs? Because only when we act from an Internal Locus of Control can we take control of our businesses and develop them toward the desired goal. In this way, we manage to take responsibility without the burden of fear and guilt that it could carry.

Of course, countless external elements are beyond our control and affect us personally and professionally. It would be naive to deny this reality. However, when we act from an Internal Locus of Control, we understand and accept that we have the power to adjust our decisions. While we cannot change external events, we can navigate them better by flexibly adjusting our decisions to allow for the best performance within our circumstances.

In short, entrepreneurs feel fear because they face uncertainty and ambiguity and are responsible for making decisions that affect their environments, businesses, employees, customers, and themselves. To successfully navigate the path of entrepreneurship and reduce the associated fear, we have two fundamental resources: reducing uncertainty through information seeking and assuming responsibility by developing an Internal Locus of Control.

The following chapters will help you better understand the different fears that entrepreneurs face and how to develop these resources to confront them.

CHAPTER 4
THE WHEEL OF 8 FEARS OF ENTREPRENEURS

"The brave man is not he who does not feel afraid, but he who conquers that fear."

Nelson Mandela

The Origin of the Model

I was motivated to take an interest in the topic of entrepreneurial fears by an article I wrote for my blog, *Eslabones de Negocio (business links),* eslabonesdenegocio.com. At that time, it was just another article. I never thought that the topic would interest me so much that I would continue to research, conduct a study, and write a book. I had no idea that I would be deeply immersed in something with layers and layers of discoveries.

When I write for my blog, I always conduct a preliminary research routine on the article's topic. At that moment, my search focused on finding and listing the main fears that entrepreneurs face. To my surprise, I found numerous and very diverse approaches and versions. Some authors mentioned three fears, others five, others ten, others twenty, and even twenty-eight (That was the longest list I found). Faced with such a profusion of variety, the exercise I decided to undertake to write the article was to list all the different fears, group them, eliminate duplicates, unify semantically equivalent terms, and then try to classify them according to larger factors or dimensions.

Based on that preliminary exercise of organizing the information other authors had discussed and proposed, I developed the initial foundation for the conceptual model I share in this book.

By organizing that long list of fears I found, I realized, first of all, that I could group all the fears into two major dimensions. Since fears, in general, are a response to the uncertainty generated by changes, I realized that these changes could occur in a person's internal conditions or the circumstances of the environment. Based on this, this conceptual model starts with a general classification of fears into two major dimensions: 1) fear of what may happen (fears of external changes) and 2) fear of how we will feel (fears of internal changes).

1. **Fears of external changes;** fears that things outside of us might happen. These are fears related to situations that change how our businesses operate or how our environment perceives or values our products or services. They are fears that "things" might happen because of some change that generates uncertainty.

2. **Fears of internal changes;** fears of feelings things. These are fears related to situations that change how we feel about our entrepreneurship or our environment. They are fears of "feeling" things or "thinking" things because of some change that generates uncertainty.

Then, I focused on the fears that fit within each of these dimensions. Based on the organization of these fears, I defined four fundamental fears within each of these dimensions to arrive at a conceptual model proposing eight fears in entrepreneurship. Four are fears of things happening, and the other four are fears of feeling things.

The Conceptual Model

Once I made the decision to research deeper into this topic beyond an article on my blog (eslabonesdenegocio.com) and began writing this book, I understood that it was essential to validate that conceptual model with empirical data. To do this, conducting research was imperative. So, in March 2023, I created a questionnaire to use as a basis for conducting a study among entrepreneurs. [1]

Based on the results, I validated some elements of the original model and adjusted others, allowing me to quantify the intensity of the various fears proposed in the conceptual model. These fears that I had initially described in the first version, which I presented in the first article on this topic on my blog, underwent some variations and adjustments. All of this was expected and desirable. It was the reason for conducting a study instead of just sticking to the initial conceptual model.

Next, I share that conceptual model as it was restructured after the results of the empirical validation with the study.

As I mentioned before, the fears faced by entrepreneurs can be initially classified into two major dimensions:

1. Fears of external events

2. Fears of internal events

Within each of these two major dimensions, we can identify a total of eight basic fears. Four are fears that respond to external events, and the other four are fears that respond to internal circumstances.

Fears of external events refer to anxieties caused by things that happen or may happen in our surroundings. These are fears that "things might happen." In contrast, fears of internal events refer to those originating from issues we can feel, anticipate, or think about internally. These are fears of "feeling" things.

---

1   In the appendix at the end of the book, you can find more details about the methodology used for data collection and the subsequent analysis of results in this study.

The model is summarized as shown in the following graph (Figure 2):

Figure 2 – Conceptual model: The wheel of 8 fears of entrepreneurs

Fears of external events refer to anxieties caused by things that happen or may happen in our surroundings. These are fears that "things might happen." In contrast, fears of internal events refer to those originating from issues we can feel, anticipate, or think about internally. These are fears of "feeling" things.

I have categorized the four fears that fall within the first dimension (fears of external events or things happening) as follows:

1. **Fear of economic losses:** This includes the fear of not generating sufficient income to cover business expenses, to provide for one's family, or even the fear of losing invested resources.

2. **Fear of change in the rules of the game:** This fear encompasses concerns about new taxes, laws, or regulations that could negatively impact the business. It also includes fears related to global economic issues on a national or international scale.

3. **Fear of competition:** This fear revolves around the idea that competitors may be stronger, offer better products and services, and potentially push the business out of the market or damage its brand, image, and reputation.

4. **Fear of operational problems:** This fear includes concerns about problems, conflicts, and disagreements with employees, partners, or even family and friends. It encompasses the fear that unforeseen issues may hinder the delivery of products and services with quality and/or on time.

The four fears that fall within the second dimension (fears of internal events or feeling things) are defined as follows:

5. **Fear of feeling incapable:** This fear relates to not having sufficient knowledge of one's business sector, lacking the expertise to make appropriate decisions, and the dread of facing unpleasant situations because of one's lack of knowledge or experience.

6. **Fear of feeling like a failure:** This fear involves the realization and acceptance of not achieving one's goals, experiencing personal failure, succumbing to a sense of defeat, and fearing the inability to manage efficiently, effectively, and decisively.

7. **Fear of feeling uncomfortable:** This fear pertains to having to make uncomfortable decisions, expose oneself to unpleasant situations, be compelled to do things that are disliked, or not feeling secure in certain actions.

8. **Fear of feeling judged:** This fear is related to concerns that family and friends may perceive the business as a bad idea, disapprove of it, doubt one's capability to succeed, or become disappointed in the entrepreneur.

Not all fears arise simultaneously. Not every entrepreneur necessarily faces all these fears, certainly not all at once, and sometimes not throughout their entrepreneurial journey. It is possible, for example, that an entrepreneur may feel the fear of feeling incapable more intensely at the beginning, while the fear of competition becomes more pronounced as the business matures and evolves. Fears are dynamic and changing, varying among different entrepreneurs and over the course of one entrepreneur's experience.

The study results allowed us to identify the relative importance of these fears in the sample group of entrepreneurs, as shown in Figures 3 and 4 below. Figure 3 displays them on the same wheel, separating external and internal fears.

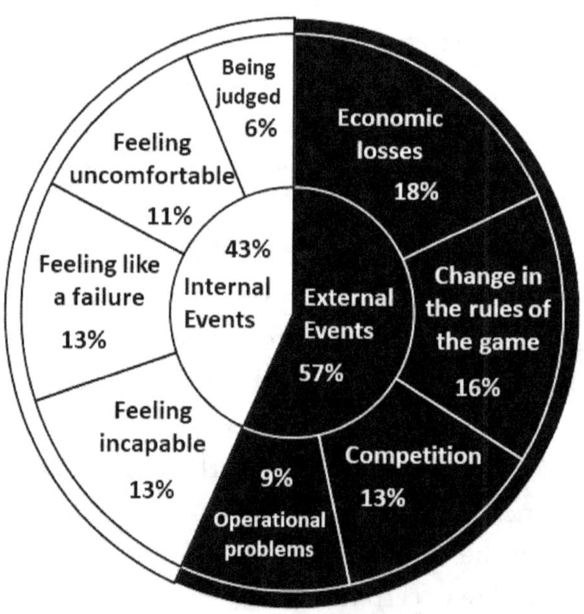

Figure 3 – Relative importance of 8 fears of entrepreneurs

Figure 4 presents the same data in descending order of importance. It's important to note that fears are dynamic and changing, influenced by market fluctuations, historical periods, geographical locations, and entrepreneurial sectors. Therefore, the relative importance of these eight fears could vary over time or manifest differently in different subgroups of entrepreneurs.

Figure 4 – Relative importance of 8 fears of entrepreneurs

According to these results, fears of external events are more relevant, or at least, they are reported as such by more entrepreneurs and with greater intensity. Among these, the most frequently reported fear is the fear of economic losses, followed by the fear of change in the rules of the game. These two are not only the top fears within this dimension but also overall. Fears of external events account for 57 percent of all fears reported by entrepreneurs.

Fears of internal events are somewhat less relevant but far from negligible. Among these, the two most frequently reported by entrepreneurs are the fear of feeling uncomfortable and the fear of feeling like a failure. Both have similar relative importance and intensity, ranking as the top two within this dimension and occupying the third and fourth positions overall. Fears of internal events make up 43 percent of all fears reported by entrepreneurs.

The Structure of the Analysis of Fears

In the following chapters, we will dig into each of these fears. I have organized the following two parts based on their relative importance as found in the study results. Therefore, we will first discuss fears originating from external events, and each of the four will have a dedicated chapter organized in the order of relative importance and intensity reported by entrepreneurs. Then, we will talk about fears originating from internal events and similarly address them in the order of relative importance and intensity found.

For each of the eight fears, the chapter will be structured as follows:

1. A conceptual discussion of what that fear is and what it entails.

2. An analysis of the effects that the presence of that fear has on your business.

3. Identification of signals that may indicate you are experiencing that specific fear.

4. Suggestions for actions that can help you successfully confront and overcome that specific fear.

I've organized the material in this way to provide a structured and practical guide with advice that you can apply successfully in your day-to-day business operations.

PART II
FEAR OF EXTERNAL CHANGES

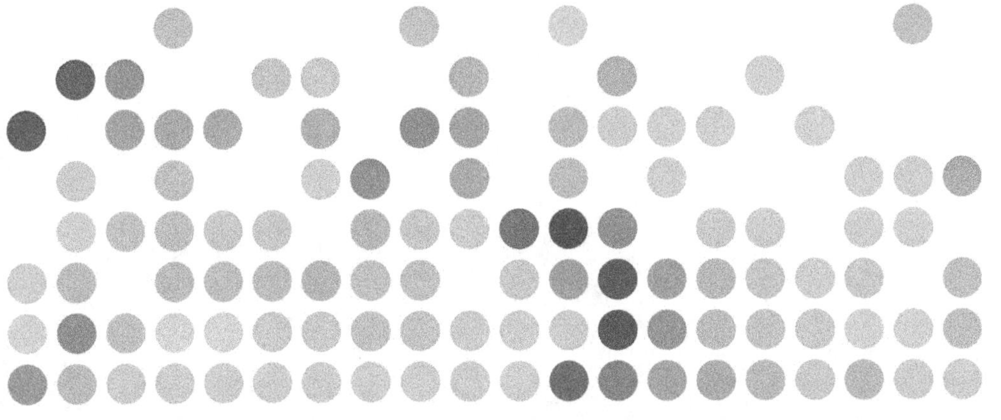

CHAPTER 5
ABOUT FEARS OF EXTERNAL CHANGES: FEAR OF THINGS HAPPENING

" You can't stop being afraid by just pretending everything that scares you isn't there."

Michael Marshall

Let's now focus on the fears I have referred to as fears of external events or fears of things happening. That is, fears of events that occur outside of us, in our environment.

Hence, the choice of Michael Marshall's quote with which I begin this chapter. When we talk about this group of four fears related to external events, we are referring to things that exist, are objective, and occur in the environment in which our business operates. We are not talking about imaginary things or things that are part of our emotional world but rather objective and real events. Since these are real situations and events, ignoring them is not an effective solution because closing our eyes to them will not make them disappear.

When we were children and were afraid of the monster under the bed, it might have been possible to ignore it and think of something else. But when we refer to concrete threats and real events that can happen or are happening, the strategy should involve accepting their existence and understanding them to confront them. In the business world, monsters do exist. They are not products of a fertile imagination.

According to the model I have developed and propose to you, fears of external events are more relevant or, at least, are reported as such by more entrepreneurs, with greater intensity than fears of internal events. Fears of external events account for 57 percent of all fears reported by entrepreneurs.

Within this large dimension of fears related to external events—
or fears of things happening—I have included four basic fears that
entrepreneurs face:

1. **Fear of financial losses:** Fear of not generating enough income
   to cover business expenses, expenses for their family, and losing
   the invested resources.

2. **Fear of change in the rules of the game:** Fear of new taxes, laws,
   or regulations that could negatively impact business. Fear of
   global economic problems and the impact of climate change.

3. **Fear of competition:** Fear that their competition is stronger,
   has better products and services, and may push them out of the
   market or damage their brand image.

4. **Fear of operational issues:** Fear of problems, conflicts, and
   disputes with employees, partners, or even family and friends.
   Fear that setbacks may prevent the delivery of quality products
   and services or meeting deadlines.

Fear of Financial Losses

The fear of financial losses is the primary fear reported by
entrepreneurs. It is the most frequent and the most intense fear. It
represents 18 percent of all internal and external fears and is reported
with an average intensity of 50 percent, the highest intensity in the study.
If all entrepreneurs had said that they "always" feel all the fears included
in this classification, the intensity would have been 100 percent, the
maximum possible. To reiterate, out of this total possible absolute fear,
an average of 50 percent was reported.

The fear of financial losses includes concerns related to money and available resources, both to keep the operation going and to cover personal and family expenses, as well as the real possibility of recovering the initial investment made in the business.

When entrepreneurs report this fear, they indicate that they fear the business going bankrupt and losing the money invested. They fear the operation will not generate enough resources to cover its costs, and additional funds will be required to continue operating. They are afraid that they will not generate enough resources to pay themselves a salary and cover all personal and family expenses within the desired quality of life or that they will not generate enough profits for the business to grow and develop.

When starting a business, resources are required, often including personal resources. Other times, external investors' resources are used. These are investors who have placed their trust in you and believe in your project, with the expectation that their investment will generate a higher return than they would get elsewhere. Whether it's your resources or those of third parties, the expectation is always that the financial result will be more favorable than what could be achieved through other forms of financial investment or business. No one starts a business intending to lose money or generate less economic benefit than they would through a different investment.

Therefore, the fear of financial losses is related to the fear that these financial expectations will not be met.

Fear of Change in the Rules of the Game

The fear of change in the rules of the game is the second most reported fear by entrepreneurs. It is the second most frequent and the second most intense. It represents 16 percent of all internal and external fears and is reported with an average intensity of 44 percent.

The fear of change in the rules of the game includes fears related to the environment in which our business operates.

When entrepreneurs report this fear, they indicate that they fear that the current conditions and assumptions on which their business operates may change. They are afraid, for example, that the government may decide to impose new taxes specifically affecting the sector in which their business operates or institute new rules and regulations that change what is possible or not within the sector. They also report the fear that the economic situation in the country (or countries) they work in may deteriorate and negatively affect operations or that the global economy may present problems or crises, changing the overall environment in which their business operates.

When starting a business, a series of economic and operational assumptions are made based on market realities at that time. However, it is clear that these conditions are beyond our control. We operate within them but have no decision-making power over certain things. And since everything is dynamic and subject to change, there is a high probability (almost a certainty) that these assumptions will change or evolve.

Depending on your business sector or the geography in which you are located, these changes may be slower or faster. But facing them at some point is inevitable. Political, economic changes; even technological and cultural changes.

Therefore, the fear of change in the rules of the game is related to the fear that these changes will occur, take us by surprise, and negatively affect us.

Fear of Competition

The fear of competition is the fifth most important fear reported by entrepreneurs. It is the fifth most frequent and the fifth most intense. It represents 13 percent of all internal and external fears and is reported with an average intensity of 35 percent.

The fear of competition includes the fear of the emergence of new competitors, products, or services, especially the possibility that they are of higher quality than what your business offers or that they better satisfy your customers' needs. Strong, aggressive competition can push you out of the market or damage your brand.

When starting a business, it will likely be in an environment with established and possibly consolidated competition. Even if you are pioneers in a segment, you may still face competition from other similar products or services, despite them not being exactly the same as yours. As markets evolve, competition also changes and transforms. You may be a leader today, but a new competitor can emerge tomorrow with more vigor and challenge your position.

Therefore, the fear of competition is related to the fear that your competitors will make better decisions and may take your market position.

Fear of Operational Problems

The fear of operational problems is the seventh most important fear reported by entrepreneurs. It is the seventh most frequent and the seventh in intensity. It represents only 9 percent of all internal and external fears and is reported with an average intensity of 28 percent. This means it has almost half the intensity of the first and most significant fear we discussed at the beginning of this chapter, namely the fear of financial losses.

The fear of operational issues includes a fear of facing problems and conflicts with employees, partners, or family and friends. It also includes a fear that issues or unforeseen circumstances may hinder or even prevent the timely delivery of quality products and services.

Every business has a set of systems and procedures. There is a way of doing things, a team of workers, and a process that is usually followed. At least, ideally, it should be like that. If we assume that we do not have this, it is evident that the likelihood of facing problems multiplies. But even if we assume that we have efficient systems and procedures that work and have properly trained work teams, there is always the possibility that something will go wrong.

You have probably heard of Murphy's Laws. It is not entirely clear where they originated, but I found out that they're often attributed to an American aerospace engineer in the 1940s, who once stated, "If there is a way for people to do something wrong, they will certainly do it." Many variations have developed, all referring to negative and fatalistic outcomes of people's efforts, in which setbacks prevail as the norm. Murphy's first law, as popularized, states, "If something can go wrong, it will."

Therefore, the fear of operational issues is exactly the fear that Murphy was right and that something could indeed go wrong. And if something goes wrong, the immediate consequence is that you must deal with the problem, find solutions, change direction, and make decisions to avoid the calamity of losing customers and money, or worse, leaving the market. Additionally, a significant part of this fear is the fear that the problems resulting from these inconveniences will not only bring operational issues but also damage relationships with valued individuals, friends, family, partners, customers, and colleagues.

In broad strokes, these are the four fears related to external events. They are fears of the possibility that things may happen in my market, environment, and business that negatively affect my ability to succeed. These external events can disrupt my procedures and plans to achieve success, resulting in economic losses, customer base losses, market share losses, damage to reputation, and ruptured relationships.

In the upcoming chapters, we will focus on each and learn to identify them. More importantly, we will learn to overcome them successfully.

CHAPTER 6
FEAR OF ECONOMIC LOSSES

*"We are more sensitive to the fear of
losing than to the desire to win."*

Joselyn Quintero

What Is and What Does the Fear of Financial Losses Entail?

We already know that the fear of financial losses is the primary fear reported by entrepreneurs. According to our study, it represents 18 percent of all internal and external fears and is reported with an average intensity of 50 percent.

Any entrepreneurial endeavor, no matter how small, requires a capital investment. We are not always talking about large sums of money. Still, almost certainly, an entrepreneurial venture will require investments in equipment, materials, licenses, services, infrastructure, and products just to get started. Entrepreneurs often use personal resources for this purpose, whether savings or some extra money they've set aside. Other times, third-party resources are used, including resources from family or friends or even external investors who have placed their trust in you and believe in your project.

When we invest money in a new business, the logical expectation is that these invested resources will generate a return greater than what we could achieve through other types of financial investments. For example, if we could earn a 5 percent annual return by leaving that money in the bank, but the financial projections for our project lead us to believe it could generate a 10 percent annual profit, we tend to think that investing it in that business is more profitable. Of course, this is an extremely simplistic explanation, as we must also consider the levels of risk involved in both options. But it gives an idea of the concept. Conversely, if the financial projections for our project indicate that we will achieve a 4 percent profit, we may be more tempted to leave those resources in the bank or restructure the business model to achieve a better profit margin.

When starting their project, many entrepreneurs fear that this investment will be lost; in other words, that there will be financial losses. This is understandably a significant barrier. In general, whenever we invest resources, whether in a project or some form of financial option, we eagerly anticipate a positive return and the growth of our capital. I mentioned this to you before, and I repeat it now: no one starts a business to lose money or generate less economic benefit than through a different investment.

The fear of financial losses entails at least three similar or related fears:

1. **Fear of losing the investment:** This involves the fear that the business does not work, and it becomes necessary to suspend or close it, resulting in the loss of both the money and effort invested in starting it. Let's say this is the most extreme case of economic failure: the total loss of the invested capital.

2. **Fear of not generating sufficient income and being unable to meet the business's financial commitments:** Generally, entrepreneurial ventures take some time to recover initial expenses and investments and generate consistent profits. There may be months with negative accounting (losses) or meager profit margins during this time. This can mean that the business does not always provide the entrepreneur with a cash flow sufficient to meet all the business's financial commitments.

3. **Fear of not generating a stable personal income:** Finally, even if the business manages to start and begins covering its expenses, having your own business implies that the income to ensure your quality of life and that of your family depends on your efforts. Being an employee guarantees you a monthly salary, but when you work on your own project, one month may be better than another. The idea is that you can generate sufficient income

consistently, but sometimes sales decline for several reasons, and perhaps the income is not enough to cover your salary.

In any case, the fear that there won't be enough money or that it will be lost leads many people to follow the advice that "A bird in the hand is worth two in the bush." They prefer to secure their current income and financial conditions, deciding not to embark on entrepreneurship rather than risk leaving their stable monthly salary and taking on the challenge of entrepreneurship independently. The fear of financial losses, then, is related to the fear that these financial expectations will not be met.

How the Fear of Financial Losses Impacts Your Business

When you experience fear of financial losses, what often happens is that you become excessively cautious with the money you invest in the business. Although this behavior may make you feel like you're in control and minimizing risk, it can negatively impact your entrepreneurship, stagnating and preventing its growth.

Some of the negative effects that the fear of financial losses can have on your business include:

1. **Lack of investment:** The fear of losses can lead you to reduce investments in areas that are crucial for your business's success, such as the development of new products, research, and development, hiring more qualified staff, or improving equipment, systems, and infrastructure.

2. **Conservative decision-making:** If you're extremely afraid of economic failure, you may adopt an overly conservative and cautious stance, avoiding risks essential for growth and

innovation. This can hinder the business's development and block your opportunities for expansion.

3. **Resistance to change:** The lack of investment and conservative decision-making can create resistance to change within the organization. Without a conducive environment for innovation and development, you and your employees may cling to existing practices and resist adopting new technologies or business strategies. You end up getting used to doing the same thing all the time. In dynamic and ever-evolving markets like the ones we experience today, this is a disadvantage for your entrepreneurship.

4. **Stagnation:** The fear of economic failure can lead you to focus excessively on short-term survival rather than seeking long-term growth opportunities. When you don't work toward a long-term vision for your business, it stagnates and you jeopardize its viability and sustainability.

5. **Loss of customer confidence:** If your customers perceive that your business is constantly concerned about losses and is unwilling to invest in its improvement or development, they may lose confidence in your company, leading to a decrease in sales and a consequent loss of your market share.

6. **Impact on employee morale:** Your fear of financial losses can affect your team and create a tense and anxious work environment. Employees may feel insecure about their jobs and fear for their financial stability because if you, as the leader, are afraid of not generating sufficient income, how much confidence can they have in the stability of their employment and the future of their professional development? This can negatively affect their morale, motivation, and commitment to work, which in turn can impact the business's overall performance or even lead them to leave your company for one they perceive as more secure and stable.

Signs You Fear Financial Losses

How can you know if you genuinely fear financial losses? How can you discern that fine line between being cautious enough not to expose your business to unnecessary risks and being so cautious that it stagnates?

Clearly, there is no one-size-fits-all answer. However, the first symptom to watch out for is the recurrence and frequency of some of the following behaviors. We all exhibit some of these symptoms from time to time. The key is to learn to distinguish between passing fear, which is just an alert, and persistent fear that causes you problems. Many of the symptoms I describe below are sometimes justified and do not necessarily represent a danger. You need to conduct a self-assessment to determine whether one or several of these behaviors are the norm for you rather than a justified temporary response.

Here are some possible ways in which this fear can manifest itself and some questions you can ask yourself. Answering affirmatively to most of them may lead you to conclude that you need to take steps to address your fear:

1. **Constant resistance to taking financial risks:** Do you tend to reject investing money in opportunities that involve some level of risk, even if they could offer potential gains? Has it been a long time since you made your last investment that involved any level of risk? Do you only have savings accounts or fixed-term deposits, even if they have a lower return than other financial investments?

2. **Obsession with control:** Do you feel the need to control every aspect of your finances? Do you struggle to delegate financial responsibilities for your business? Does it stress you to see minor variations between budget forecasts and your business's actual performance?

3. **Excessive worry about the future:** Are you constantly thinking about the possibility of your business going bankrupt? Do you fear not having enough funds to cover expenses for the next month, quarter, semester, or year?

4. **Tendency to avoid acquisitions and investments:** Do you always look for excuses to postpone investments in equipment, technology, or systems that could benefit your business's operations? Are you still waiting for the "perfect moment" to make these purchases?

5. **Anxiety and stress:** Do you have difficulty sleeping or concentrating due to thoughts of pending payments? Do you frequently regret the decision to start your own business?

Action Steps to Face and Overcome the Fear of Financial Losses

Like all the fears entrepreneurs face, which we will analyze throughout this book, you can overcome the fear of financial losses so that it does not prevent you from making favorable decisions for your entrepreneurship while protecting your investment. You should set two goals: 1) act positively, avoiding becoming paralyzed, i.e., increase the probability of a successful investment, and 2) at the same time, be responsible for the level of risk you assume, i.e., reduce the likelihood of losing the investment. It's bad to become paralyzed due to fear and miss out on opportunities that could be good. But it's also harmful to ignore the fear and plunge in without taking proper precautions.

What can you do to reduce the fear of financial losses? Below are some strategies that can help you:

1. **Be better informed:** The best way to reduce the fear of financial loss is to minimize the uncertainty surrounding your investment and business. To the extent that there is less uncertainty, the decisions made are more likely to succeed, increasing the chances that the business will be profitable rather than incur losses. Let's be realistic; there's always some risk. The goal is not to completely eliminate risk because that's not possible. The goal should be to reduce the risk to the lowest possible level.

   We've previously mentioned that fear is generated by uncertainty. When we don't know what might happen due to our decisions, we fear making those decisions. Therefore, the answer is simple: if we can reduce uncertainty levels, fear will decrease because we will have a clearer understanding of the probabilities of success and failure.

   How do you reduce this uncertainty? The only answer here is information. The more information you have, and the higher its quality, the better equipped you'll be to predict the possible consequences of your decisions. When you're afraid to make decisions due to uncertainty, you should strive to read, research, ask, and seek all available information that helps make the future picture less uncertain.

2. **Have a well-structured financial plan:** It's impossible to run your business without precise numbers. I know this is one of the most challenging aspects for many entrepreneurs, as it's not their area of expertise in most cases. In fact, I believe that this lack of understanding of financial basics is one of the main factors that generate this significant fear in entrepreneurs. Throughout the life of my blog, Eslabones de Negocio, I've interviewed quite a few small and micro-entrepreneurs. One of the questions I often ask them is about their main challenge when deciding to start their businesses, the biggest obstacle they had to overcome. Most of the

entrepreneurs I've interviewed confess that their main challenge was financial management.

Your financial plan should estimate all the numbers that will affect your business's finances: sales projections, fixed cost calculations, variable cost calculations, pricing of your products or services, estimation of the resources you need to start, expected profit estimation, estimation of the time it will take to recover the investment and start generating profits, and sources of financing (if needed). The less you leave to chance and the more definition you insist on, the lower the risk of making mistakes and losing money.

3. **Ensure that your price calculation includes all costs:** A common concern for many entrepreneurs is calculating the price at which they will offer their products or services. There's often a lack of understanding of all the implications involved in this calculation.

It's crucial to calculate the prices at which you should sell your products or services accurately. It's common for deficits in businesses to result from charging the wrong price, one that doesn't reflect the reality of costs, isn't competitive for your market, or doesn't align with the benefits you offer. Whether the price is too low or too high compared to the right price, it can negatively affect you.

Basically, your price includes two elements: 1) all your costs + 2) a profit margin.

It sounds simple, doesn't it? So why is it sometimes so complicated to calculate the price? Because the calculation of costs involves many variables. If you leave some of them out, your cost will be unrealistic, and therefore, your price will not be adequate.

The idea is that each unit of product or service you offer should incorporate, in some proportion, all the costs you incur. This includes all types of raw materials you require, expendable materials, fixed costs, personnel expenses (including your own salary), external professionals, marketing, sales, and advertising expenses, travel and transportation expenses, financial expenses, other expenses, and at least a 5 percent allowance for unexpected costs. You'd be surprised that many entrepreneurs are unaware of how to incorporate all these costs into their price calculations.

4. **Understand your market:** Another critical element to making sound financial estimates and avoiding economic losses that hinder entrepreneurs is to have realistic and precise sales estimates. Don't estimate your potential sales based solely on what you'd like to achieve. Try to estimate what's feasible with the resources you have, and if they are not sufficient to generate the necessary sales, consider increasing your resources or changing your systems. Force yourself to seek all the information that helps you understand your market and define your business model according to your consumer, the channels you operate in, and your product or service. Conducting small-scale test markets that allow you to understand your customers' potential reactions and the acceptance of your product or service can be very useful.

5. **Seek support from professionals specializing in the field:** If necessary, don't hesitate to seek accounting and financial assistance from professionals to ensure the quality of your analysis. To save on specialized advice at the beginning, we often engage in inappropriate investments or make financial decisions with a high likelihood of failure. If you don't come from a financial or accounting background or don't know your market's figures well enough to make accurate and precise estimates, it's best to hire a specialist who can provide objective and professional support.

6. **Always cushion the falls:** It's advisable to have sufficient financial reserve to cover your personal and family expenses until the entrepreneurship starts generating profits. If possible, even a reserve that can cover the business's operating costs for the necessary time until the investment starts paying off. If you have those resources, you automatically reduce anxiety and fear surrounding the business's success, at least during the initial months of work when you may not generate enough income.

   Additionally, in your budgets, always account for a margin for contingencies. I've always applied a 5 percent margin for unexpected expenses, but depending on your business sector, you may require more or less room for unforeseen events and estimation errors. Don't fall into the temptation of setting a margin of error too high, as you risk being lax and not rigorous enough with your expenses.

   If you only have the initial investment and expect the project to generate money immediately to cover your costs and ensure your income, you're likely walking on turbulent waters and assuming more risk than recommended.

7. **Continuously monitor:** Having a financial plan is not enough. You must continuously monitor your income and expenses in detail and compare them with your estimates. Do this over short periods (no longer than a month) to be able to see discrepancies between your estimates and the actual execution and take corrective action promptly.

   Prepare Excel spreadsheets or another suitable system in which you meticulously record key performance indicators for your business. Track your sales, expenses, and profits month after month and use that information to make on-the-fly decisions, prevent problems, and avoid financial losses. If you don't closely validate your estimates and update them as you go, you won't realize whether you are or aren't achieving your goals and whether you can or can't recover your investment and start generating profits within the expected time frame.

8. **Accept that some losses are inevitable:** Understand one reality: it's almost certain that any business venture will incur some losses at some point, especially at the beginning. It's part of the learning curve.

   What's important is not that this doesn't happen but that you plan for it and estimate it as accurately as possible before starting. With proper estimates, you can accurately determine how many months you need to be in the red, when you will start generating profits, and how long it will take to recover the investment and effectively generate additional income.

9. **Understand seasonality in your business sector:** Many business sectors flourish during certain times of the year and slow down during others due to the nature of their activities. As you get to know and understand these seasonal trends in your sector, you'll feel more in control and calm. During seasons when sales may decline, you can prepare to take advantage of the busier seasons.

CHAPTER 7
FEAR OF CHANGE IN THE RULES OF THE GAME

"Nothing is permanent except change."

Heraclitus

What is and What Does the Fear of Change in the Rules of the Game Entail?

The fear of change in the rules of the game is the second fear reported by entrepreneurs. It is the second most common and the second most intense. It represents 16 percent of all internal and external fears and is reported with an average intensity of 44 percent.

The fear of change in the rules of the game includes the fear that changes may occur in the conditions in which our business operates. When entrepreneurs report this fear, they indicate that they are afraid that the current conditions and assumptions on which their business is based may change. They fear, for example, that the government may create new taxes that specifically affect the sector in which their entrepreneurship operates or that new rules and regulations may be instituted to change what is possible within the sector. They also report the fear that the economic situation in the country (or countries) in which they operate may deteriorate and negatively affect operations or that the global economy may present problems or crises, changing the overall environment in which their entrepreneurship is placed.

The reality is that our environment is constantly changing, as expressed in the quote by Heraclitus at the beginning of this chapter. Just three years ago, we unexpectedly faced a pandemic due to COVID-19, which surely no one had in their business plan. For almost two years, we have witnessed a war with Russia's invasion of Ukrainian territory. These complex global situations affect, and will continue to affect, our markets. It doesn't matter how far geographically we are from the conflict zone or how distant this reality may seem from our own micro-entrepreneurship. All of this has a global impact on our economies and, consequently, alters our markets. This situation triggers the fear of market changes that we cannot control but which can affect our businesses as the assumptions on which we have developed our plans change.

The examples of global changes I just mentioned, such as pandemics and wars, are examples of significant changes that affect most businesses to a greater or lesser extent. However, we also constantly face changes that may be more specific to your business sector or reality. I'm referring to things like the emergence of new competitors who could displace or outperform your competitive advantages, new regulations and taxes that could require adjustments to your business model, and new technologies. Even the emergence of substitute products and services or passing fads and trends could potentially push you out of the market.

All these market changes, in one way or another, generate fear. This fear arises mainly because it creates uncertainty about our future. It clouds our vision of what's to come and, as a result, increases the levels of risk. When the rules are clear and stable, we have a better idea of what can happen, and we can make the necessary preparations to deal with all our costs or market and sector conditions. But when the rules are changed, at least for a while, and until we learn the new rules to participate in the unfamiliar environment, we feel like they moved out from under us. We don't want to act because we don't know what might happen. Perhaps our planned resources are not enough because new costs have emerged. Or maybe we don't know how to respond to the latest technologies that the competition has implemented.

We know that fear is triggered as a reaction to the perception of a potential threat. If we don't know what will happen, and there's a high risk of negative consequences, our businesses feel threatened. Consequently, we feel fear.

When we start a business, we start based on a specific situation that we already know. There is a specific situation at a personal level, at the level of our sector, country, continent, and globally. We project our business plan into a future based on assumptions developed from what, in our judgment, is most likely to happen. Whenever we plan, we make some kind of projection or estimation. To the extent that the assumptions on which we base those predictions are met, our decisions are more likely to be successful.

We start our business with a series of economic and operational assumptions based on the realities of the market at that time. Economic decisions, operational structure, and processes are created based on these assumptions because that's what we know. However, it's clear that these conditions are beyond our control. Although we operate in a certain environment, we have no decision-making power over specific elements. And since everything is dynamic and subject to change, there is a high probability (almost a certainty) that these assumptions will eventually evolve.

Depending on your business sector or the geography in which you are located, these variations may be slower or faster. But facing them is inevitable at some point.

The fear of change in the rules of the game, then, has to do with the fear that these alterations will occur, catch us off guard, and negatively affect us.

How the Fear of Change in the Rules of the Game Impacts Your Business

When you fear the rules of the game may change, you will likely be very conservative in your decisions and operations. To mitigate exposure to uncertainties, you may choose to operate within the familiar, in the most stable environment, minimizing the potential for variations. This way, you minimize the likelihood of encountering changes.

The main problem this behavior brings is you are likely to operate within narrower boundaries because exploring new horizons progressively increases the likelihood of facing changes. Your decisions remain within predictable patterns. Consequently, the possibility of innovation and growth is affected.

Some of the negative effects that the fear of change in the rules of the game can have on your business are as follows:

1. **Limited innovation:** The fear of facing changes in your environment can lead you to avoid them internally in the company. Any innovation may potentially expose you to unknown factors, and innovations generally occur in market sectors that are dynamic and evolving. If you are afraid of exposing yourself to these changing sectors, you will try to preserve what you have rather than innovate.

2. **Lack of growth:** If you do not innovate and are unwilling to expose yourself to changing and developing sectors, you may fall behind your competitors. This can limit the growth and development of your business.

3. **Resistance to change:** If you fear changes in the market, you may feel comfortable with how you are doing things, regardless of whether better alternatives are available. You may become

resistant to change or adopting innovative technologies or practices.

4. **Lack of flexibility:** When you fear and resist change, you are generally inflexible. In physical terms, when something is not flexible and is subjected to opposing forces , it most likely breaks and suffers structural damage. On the other hand, a flexible structure yields and adapts to external forces, adjusting to prevent breaking. In the business world, we can take this lesson almost literally. If an organization is rigid (in terms of procedures, values, systems, and beliefs), environmental changes and opposing forces result in negative consequences and often lead to a breakdown.

5. **Excessive focus on your competition:** If you fear changes in the market, you may be overly concerned about what your competitors are doing, which can prevent you from focusing on your own strategy. You may spend too much time analyzing the competition and trying to imitate them instead of focusing on customer satisfaction and value creation.

Signs You Fear Change in the Rules of the Game

How can you tell that you fear change in the rules of the game and the market in which your entrepreneurship operates? Below, I'll list some possible ways in which this fear can manifest and some questions you can ask yourself. Answering "yes" to most of these questions may lead you to conclude that you need to take steps to address this fear:

1. **Resistance to change:** Do you tend to reject proposals for changes made by your employees or customers? Do you tend to question any suggestion and easily find a "good reason" (or rather, an

excuse?) not to implement it? Do you prefer known systems and procedures?

2. **Lack of efficient sources of information:** Are you generally the last to hear about new technologies that affect your business sector? Do you need your legal or tax advisor to call and inform you about a new regulation? Do your employees inform you about market news? Do you find it difficult to obtain historical information about your customers' behavior?

3. **Surprised by your competition:** Do you discover the new products offered by your competitors when you're shopping at the supermarket, see new ads, or see them at events and conventions? Does it surprise you that your competition's sales figures have increased and are negatively impacting your business?

4. **Adaptation difficulties:** When asked for changes or adjustments to the products or services you offer, do you require much time, effort, and resources to implement them? Do you feel anxious about the possibility of having to modify current procedures? Do you do things the same way you did ten years ago?

Action Steps to Face and Overcome the Fear of Change in the Rules of the Game

How do entrepreneurs face the fear of change in the rules of the game in the market? It depends largely on our own planning and study efforts.

If we plan for a certain future, the key to successfully confronting the fear that this future may differ from our expectations and negatively affect us lies in two crucial elements. The first is our ability to stay informed and up to date with the necessary information that alerts us timely to potential changes. The second is our ability to develop highly flexible structures, business models, and processes with the possibility of making rapid adjustments as market changes demand.

If we are attentive to potential changes and have the ability to react, we feel in control and capable of responding; consequently, fear diminishes.

What can you do to reduce this fear of market changes? How can you increase the feeling that you are in control? Here are some strategies that can help:

1. **Develop tolerance for ambiguity:** It's essential that we learn to coexist harmoniously with ambiguity. Uncertainty is inevitable in our personal and professional journey. Since it is a permanent companion, it's a good idea to try to get along with it because it will always be with us. It's better to have it as an ally rather than an enemy. And, as with anyone we must live with, we'll fare better the more we get to know it. Developing greater tolerance for ambiguity involves learning to stay in control in the face of uncertainty despite the discomfort that not having answers or not knowing where you're headed can cause.

2. **Maintain an updated base of continuous information:** It's vital to have varied, diverse, and reliable sources of information. You need general information about the economy and politics of the geographies that affect your business, specific details on the sector in which you operate, and internal information about your own entrepreneurship. As you can see, you need information from the general to the specific. The more reliable data you have, the more precise your outlook will be. Think of information as prescription glasses that eliminate the fog that prevents you from seeing ahead. When you're nearsighted and walking towards a

distant goal, the path and the goal can appear blurry. However, when you wear your glasses, you see more clearly and can walk confidently because you have a better view of your destination and the path that will lead you there. Information works the same way; it clears the fog and turbulence and focuses your vision on the future. With that, you can better plan your strategic actions.

3. **Foster efficient and consistent communication with customers, suppliers, employees, and even colleagues in business or professional associations.** It's incredible how much valuable information you can obtain by asking and talking to the other actors involved in your business environment. You should focus on listening, seeing, and reading everything that can provide relevant information. It's in your best interest to keep updated databases. You should make an active effort to converse with customers, employees, and suppliers on a regular basis.

4. **Achieve flexibility in operations and strategies to easily adapt to market changes.** When structures are not flexible, being forced to change direction can break them. The same happens with companies. When your processes and company's structures are too rigid, change and adaptation are slow, preventing you from reacting to market changes. You must try to develop a highly flexible business with a high capacity for adaptation and speed of reaction. This way, even if you can only see ahead in shorter periods (because market changes are very rapid), you can react and adjust to respond adequately and for your benefit.

5. **Develop analytical thinking.** Only when we have a clear understanding of a situation can we use it as support for our decision-making. Knowledge involves more than just having information. It requires analysis and integration. Most of the news that comes to us, which can help us build a relatively clear picture of the future situation, is isolated "data." This is the most

basic element from which we can build solid knowledge. Data, being the most basic link, must be transformed into information, which, in turn, must be transformed into knowledge. Only when we have turned data into knowledge can we effectively say that we understand a situation. It also serves as a basis for making decisions and planning.

CHAPTER 8
FEAR OF COMPETITION

"It is nice to have valid competition; it pushes you to do better."

Gianni Versace

What is and What Does the Fear of Competition Entail?

The fear of competition is the fifth most important among the fears reported by entrepreneurs. It's the fifth most frequent and the fifth most intense. It represents 13 percent of all internal and external fears and manifests with an average intensity of 35 percent.

Unless our entrepreneurship is a monopoly, competition will always exist. Being afraid of it is normal because, since it doesn't depend on us, we have no control over its decisions or actions, which leads to uncertainty about the future dynamics in our sector. And once again, we return to the same concept we've repeated several times: uncertainty and lack of control generate fear. Why? Because it makes us vulnerable and leads us to think about the danger of our competitor's actions negatively affecting the success of our business.

The fear of competition manifests in two forms:

1. **Fear that the competition will displace and surpass you because they have better products or services:** This includes the fear that new competitors, new products, or new services may emerge, especially the fear that they might be superior in quality to what your entrepreneurship offers or better satisfy your customers'

needs. Strong, aggressive competition can push you out of the market or damage your reputation.

2. **Fear that the competition will copy you:** This includes the fear that any initiative or innovation you take might be discovered by your competition and implemented in the market before you have the opportunity to do it.

When you start a business, it inevitably occurs within an environment with established competition. Even if you are pioneers in a segment, you may still face competition from other similar products or services, despite them not being exactly the same as yours. As markets evolve, so does competition. You might be a leader today, but a new competitor could emerge more forcefully tomorrow.

Competition isn't inherently bad; in fact, it's necessary and positive. Competition stimulates innovation because it fosters the need for improvement, leading to overall market, product, and service enhancements for consumers. Additionally, competition allows for better price control and stabilization, forcing companies to become more efficient in offering high-quality products and services at reasonable prices. When there's no competition, as in the case of a monopoly, the company offering the product or service has significant power and much greater freedom to act arbitrarily, often negatively affecting customers and consumers.

Thus, competition provides a frame of reference and presents challenges and opportunities, ultimately empowering the consumer or customer, who has the final say in selecting products and services that best meet their needs, with the best quality and price.

Since competition puts the power in the hands of the consumer, it instills fear in us when we're uncertain about the likelihood of consumers preferring our products. We feel threatened because we think clients might prefer another brand or company participating in the market over us, resulting in a loss of market share and revenue.

How the Fear of Competition Impacts Your Business

The fear of competition negatively affects our entrepreneurship because it shifts our focus outward from our business rather than inward. It distracts us, making us more concerned about other businesses than our own. This can lead to making decisions based on the actions of others rather than our vision. In essence, what primarily happens is that this fear turns your entrepreneurship into a reactive company rather than a proactive one. If a company constantly worries about what its competitors are doing, it may lose sight of its strategy and value proposition. Instead of focusing on improving its products, services, and customer experience, the company may expend most of its energy and resources trying to keep up with the competition.

Some of the negative effects that the fear of competition can have on your business include:

1. **Reactive behavior:** When you make decisions out of fear of what your competition might do, you are essentially reacting to events or circumstances after they happen. Developing a reactive behavior leads you to become more passive and wait for things to happen before acting. You start basing your actions on external demands or pressures, and you may feel overwhelmed or overrun by circumstances. When you behave this way, your company suffers and is negatively affected, becoming vulnerable to whatever happens in your target market's environment.

2. **Follower instead of innovator:** The fear of what your competition might do leads you to wait for them to act first before following

suit. While this guarantees greater safety since you can already see the market consequences of your competition's decisions, it negatively affects you as it turns your brand into a follower, diminishing your leadership. You allow your competitors to take the lead. Your fear then places your company in a follower position, limiting possibilities for development, growth, and differentiation.

3. **Stagnation:** The fear of what your competition might do can lead to paralysis. When you freeze, you stop acting, become complacent, and avoid taking risks. You may get stuck in traditional ways of doing things. This limits your company's ability to adapt to market changes and stay relevant. There's a risk that this resistance to change may become part of your business's organizational culture, and your employees may also feel threatened by competitors, thereby resisting innovation and adopting new strategies or technologies at the cost of your company's competitiveness, which should be the cornerstone of your business.

4. **Excessive secrecy:** The fear of your competition getting ahead of you can lead to extreme secrecy. While it's necessary to maintain high levels of discretion and confidentiality around key innovations in your business, as they can largely constitute competitive advantages, it's important to trust your team so they can work in the same direction and develop synergy. Excessive secrecy (based on an inability to trust) can damage transparency, communication, workplace culture, and your business's responsiveness.

5. **Lack of confidence:** The fear of competition can undermine your company's confidence in its abilities and capabilities. It can make your company feel insecure about its position in the market and believe it's always at a disadvantage compared to its competitors.

This lack of confidence can easily be transmitted throughout the entire workforce and may lead you to make conservative decisions and avoid taking necessary risks for growth.

Signs You Fear Competition

How can you tell that you are afraid of your competition? Sometimes, there can be a very fine line between the need to stay alert to market changes and be flexible to adjust course in line with trends and the fearful, reactive response to every threatening move from your competition. On the one hand, you're told that you should be alert and prepared for change, but on the other hand, you're told not to decide reactively. I understand that it can be confusing. Ultimately, the key is learning to be flexible and adapt to your market while always keeping your true north clear. In other words, you should adjust the path you travel, but not your destination.

Here are some possible ways in which this fear can manifest itself and some questions you can ask yourself. Answering "yes" to most of them may lead you to conclude that you need to address this fear:

1. **Defensive strategies:** Do you easily change your strategy whenever there are developments in your market? Do you react defensively to every threat from your competition? When you learn about an innovation from your competition, do you immediately think it will take away your market share? Do you change your company's key objectives right away? Do you feel your company is not trying to differentiate itself from your competitors and is not looking for ways to stand out in the market? Do you tend to want to imitate what your competitors have done successfully?

2. **Constant negative criticism of your competition:** Do you often seek to downplay the strengths of your competition? Do you find

it difficult to acknowledge that your competition is doing well? Do you often catch yourself wishing for your competition to fail with their new idea, that the innovation they just offered doesn't resonate with consumers? Do you feel envious or resentful when your competition achieves any success?

3. **Insecurity and lack of confidence:** Do you frequently think that your value proposition is inferior to that of your competition? Do you doubt the ability of your products and services to adequately meet your customers' needs? Do you frequently adjust your products and services to copy attributes you think are your competition's strengths? Do you find it difficult to try things that your competitors haven't tried yet? Are you more comfortable operating within the traditional procedures you already know than seeking new ideas? Does the success of your competitors make you feel insecure about your own capabilities and skills?

4. **Obsession with competition:** Are you constantly focused on what your competitors are doing? Do you regularly compare your products, services, prices, and strategies with those of your competitors? Do you invest a disproportionate amount of time and energy monitoring the activities and movements of your competition?

Action Steps to Face and Overcome the Fear of Competition

A simple way to understand this fear is to place it in the context of sports competition. You can probably relate to the example if you've ever participated in a competitive sport or know someone who has. Imagine you are part of a soccer team, and the coach has registered the team to participate in a tournament. Feeling fear when you're about to face other teams is expected. When do you feel the most fear? It's when you don't know the level of play of your opponent or when you're certain that they are very good, better than your team. How does the coach handle this situation? By seeking information that allows understanding of the tactics and strategies of the opposing team and by training your team to consolidate its strengths and overcome its weaknesses. The more you feel your team has the skill to win the game, the less fear you will experience. You achieve this by knowing the opposing teams and through preparation and hard work.

Well, that same formula is what we should use when we face this fear of competition in our business. How can we do it? Here are some strategies that can help you overcome this fear:

1. **Know and analyze your competition:** Just like the coach in our example observes and analyzes the opposing teams' tactics and strategies, you must actively make a great effort to get to know your competition. Without obsessively pursuing them, you need to know the key players in your market sector.

   And not only that, you must also find out why consumers prefer them. Is it because they offer a better quality producer service? Because they better satisfy their needs? Because they have a more attractive price? Because they are more readily available and easy to find? Because consumers are more familiar with the brands? Because they are accustomed to using them? The list of possible reasons is vast. It's necessary to understand what consumers perceive in your competition and why they prefer them. To do this, you can use various strategies, from informal conversations with your consumers and suppliers, database analysis, and social media content to conducting formal, extensive, valid, and comprehensive market studies.

The better you know your competition and understand their strengths and weaknesses, the better you can prepare to face them and make consumers prefer your brand or company, leading to market growth.

2. **Provide added value to your customers:** Get into the habit of listening to your customers. The only way to adequately meet their needs is by knowing them well. It's important to discover which of your customers' needs are not being met by the current offerings. To do this, you must learn to listen before speaking and remember to ask the right questions. The challenge is to go beyond the need itself and understand the emotional trigger that activates it.

In general, we prefer talking over listening. Listening feels like a more passive attitude that places the spotlight on others. Entrepreneurs like to lead and direct the conversation. We're not always good listeners. The more we try to speak less and listen more, the better opportunities we'll have to understand our consumers more deeply. Listening is not passive behavior; it requires attention, analytical ability, and synthesis.

Ask the right questions. Don't ask them:

- What new products do you need?
- What additional benefits to the ones you have would you like to have?
- What can I offer you to improve your experience?

Instead, ask them:

- Which unmet needs would you like to identify and address that are currently not being attended to?

- Is there anything you dislike about the current products or services?
- What motivates you to use those products or services?
- What satisfies you the most about those products or services?

3. **Focus on your strengths:** Kevin Stirtz, a digital marketing expert, speaker, and author of several books, says, *"Know what your customers want most and what your company does best. Focus on where those two meet."* Instead of trying to see what your competition is doing for your customer, concentrate on discovering and consolidating your strengths.

   It will always be much easier to leverage what you excel at rather than improvise on what you don't excel at just because your competition does it.

   Of course, this doesn't mean you should close yourself off to the possibility of learning new things and developing new strengths. What I want to make clear is that to stand out, it's much more efficient to start with what you do best.

4. **Focus on your niche:** There's a saying that goes, "You're not a golden coin to be liked by everyone." It means that it's impossible to be everyone's favorite. When your potential customer base is very broad, it's challenging to offer benefits that satisfy all needs. Consequently, you'll end up not satisfying anyone.

   You've probably heard another saying, "He who wants too much doesn't catch anything." I suggest you apply this concept very strictly. Even though the temptation is to define a broad audience so that many people can buy from you, the reality is that the broader your reach, the more difficult it is to hit the mark.

5. **Seek differentiation:** Don't copy your competition. If the consumer prefers them because they are good at achieving "A," don't try to copy them and offer "A" as well. Look for which other benefit "B" your customer might be requiring that the current competition does not satisfy and focus on developing a product or service that is different, innovative, and has the potential to be preferred by your target market because it is unique.

6. **Strive for excellence:** As expressed in the quote by Gianni Versace at the beginning of this chapter, competition is a driving force for improvement. When you compete in a market with many high-quality players, you must constantly surpass yourself and improve through innovation, making processes more efficient, and ensuring quality.

Just like in the example of the soccer team, where the coach prepares the team to improve their level of play every day, you must work every day to enhance your offering and your business. The better you are, the more confident you will feel in your capabilities, and as a result, you will reduce the fear that your competition can surpass you.

CHAPTER 9
FEAR OF OPERATIONAL PROBLEMS

"The best approach is to dig out and eliminate problems where they are assumed not to exist."

Shigeo Shingo

What Is and What Does the Fear of Operational Problems Entail?

Every operation can fail, even the most planned and perfect one. It's a risk that always exists. And this possibility that something might go wrong in the process, or the planned scheme, is the last of the four fears of things happening: the fear of operational problems.

When we talk about the fear of operational problems, we are referring to the fear that arises from the possibility of facing a situation where the pieces do not fit properly, or at least not as we had envisioned. This potential situation can negatively affect our ability to deliver our product or service with the desired quality, on the promised schedule, or at the correct cost.

The fear of operational problems is when entrepreneurs believe failures and omissions may occur in the processes, leading to errors and losses. It also includes the fear of facing problems and conflicts with employees, partners, or family and friends. In short, it's the fear of facing any inconvenience that disrupts the ideal process.

The fear of operational problems ranks seventh in importance among the fears reported by entrepreneurs. It is the seventh most frequent and the seventh most intense, representing only 9 percent of all internal and external fears and occurring with an average intensity of 28 percent. This means it has less than half the intensity of the first and strongest fear we saw earlier, the fear of economic losses.

This fear is related to the fear of failure. It affects entrepreneurs and ventures and anyone in any professional and personal setting. In the most extreme cases, which often require professional assistance, it is known as "Atychiphobia," defined as the *"irrational, persistent, and unjustified fear of making mistakes or being wrong."* In less extreme cases, this fear of failure is known as *"anticipatory anxiety"* and refers to the *"unease or distress generated by thinking about the possibility of failure or error in a task or project we must face in the future."*

In this case, as well as with the other fears we are analyzing, we are not referring to extreme phobias because they require professional assistance but to situations of mild discomfort or anxiety that can be controlled by developing specific skills but still affect the entrepreneur's performance.

To overcome this fear, we must first assess the problems and accept that problems will always arise. Part of an entrepreneur's day-to-day life involves solving problems, sometimes one after another. If you want to avoid possible problems, it's better not to start a business.

Every business has a set of systems and procedures. There is a way of doing things, a team, a process that is usually followed. At least, ideally, it should be that way. If we don't have this in place, it's clear that the chances of problems multiply. But even if we assume that we have efficient systems and procedures that work and teams that are adequately trained, there is always the possibility that something will fail.

This is one of the fears that we have the most control over. There are many measures we can take to prevent potential operational problems and many measures we can have in place to resolve them if they arise.

Of course, there is always the possibility of unforeseen events, from issues within our business (such as the possibility of equipment breaking or failing, people who we rely on who get sick, personal problems, or quitting) to local problems in the area where we operate our business (strikes, political or economic issues, natural disasters) and even global problems affecting all markets (such as the recent pandemic we have experienced, wars, and global economic crises).

Although these unforeseen events can always occur, we cannot be paralyzed. It is always possible to make provisions to minimize a negative impact or enable a quick recovery.

Other situations related to this fear include relationship and communication problems. Although they are not operational problems per se, they still affect operations, efficiency, and productivity. When we fear conflict or damaging our personal or business relationships, we often remain silent and yield rather than defend our opinions. We avoid expressing ideas that may contradict someone else. We avoid imposing our viewpoints, even when we are convinced that our position is correct and could benefit our business. Problems arise when there is tension between what both parties want, between what one party requests and what the other is willing to give, between what each party considers appropriate procedures, and the values assumed to prevail in decision-making.

Having to carry out a project can prevent us from being on good terms with everyone. Sometimes, we must make decisions that others do not like, delegate tasks, accept the learning curve, be leaders and manage personnel, demand from suppliers, handle customer problems, and a myriad of situations where we expose the harmony of our relationships, which, if mishandled, can lead to ruptures.

Conflicts in themselves are not negative. Depending on how we handle them, they can even be positive and contribute to progress and growth in an organization. Differences of opinion allow us to compare ideas and weigh the pros and cons of each option. They lead us to evaluate scenarios we might not have considered otherwise, broadening our opportunities.

How the Fear of Operational Problems Impacts Your Business

You probably agree that it's frustrating to dedicate time to any project and realize that the pieces you have worked on separately don't fit well when you put everything together. If you enjoy crafts or DIY, you may have experienced this firsthand when assembling or fixing things in your home. It's when screws and nuts don't fit well, when the holes that are supposed to align are a couple of millimeters off, or when the pieces of the dress you're sewing don't close perfectly at the seam.

This same feeling of frustration transfers to our entrepreneurial ventures when what one team has worked on is not entirely compatible with what another team has worked on. When the numbers don't add up as they should. When the schedule experiences delays, causing a loss of time in the process.

This leads to having to redo work, with the consequent increase in costs and even delays in delivery commitments. All of this translates into costly economic losses.

Being repeatedly exposed to such episodes in our professional and daily lives can impact our willingness to undertake projects because it can lead us to fear that, once we are fully operational with our project, we will have to face painful operational problems.

So, what happens in our businesses when we fear facing these problems? How does it affect us? We are not analyzing how the operational problem itself affects us but rather how much fear we feel about the possibility of it happening. And that opens five windows, namely:

1. **Impatience and Intolerance:** When we fear that problems may occur, we may be excessively sensitive, causing us great stress and distress even over the smallest failure. If we approach problems with stress, instead of seeking solutions, we look for culprits and tend to be impatient and intolerant of those who may have made mistakes or whom we consider responsible. This can lead to developing an organizational culture of "terror" in which our collaborators will also fear making mistakes because they will expose themselves to our negative reactions. This can be counterproductive as it may lead to making more mistakes due to nervousness and lack of confidence or, worse, hiding errors to avoid negative reactions. This leads us to the second negative effect.

2. **Hidden Errors:** If we fear that problems may occur and convey that to our teams, they will likely try to hide errors and inconveniences or solve them their own way, which may not be the ideal solution for the company and/or the customer. This can lead to us unknowingly delivering subpar products and services. Consequently, the customer discovers the error instead of addressing it before delivery, negatively impacting the company's image and customer trust.

3. **Low Resilience:** When we fear failure and problems, we may feel discouraged every time we face them because we will approach them with a bad attitude and disposition. This will make it more difficult to overcome each small failure or inconvenience, learn from it, correct it, and move forward.

Resilience is the ability to face problems and overcome obstacles. But it goes beyond that; it's not just about overcoming the adverse situation. Being resilient means that when we return to normal, we return stronger, with increased potential and deeper learning. In this sense, resilience is a process of growth because it forces us to develop our abilities to face difficulties and emerge with greater competencies.

For entrepreneurs, resilience is especially important because we face many pressures, unforeseen events, and adversities. Many ventures fail in the early years for not having developed the ability to navigate these turbulent waters properly, adjust course, and move forward.

4. **Low Productivity:** If you fear failure, you will be overly cautious, which may result in working slower than necessary. Being cautious and careful is not a bad thing; on the contrary. However, if taken to the extreme, it can unnecessarily lengthen the time it takes to complete a process, which can negatively affect your business's productivity. You produce less, and as a result, your costs increase (slower = more time required = higher time cost).

5. **Lack of Innovation:** Once again, the innovation capacity of your business is negatively affected by fear (notice that several of the fears we have analyzed so far affect the company's innovation capacity). If you are afraid of facing problems of any kind, you may feel much more comfortable staying in familiar and proven territories over venturing into uncharted waters and forging new paths. Every innovation brings with it the possibility of new problems that you must anticipate, address, and overcome. Little by little, you will start discarding new ideas, and your company will lag behind the competition.

Signs You Fear Operational Problems

How can you tell if you are afraid to face operational problems and various inconveniences in your entrepreneurial venture? Once again, a fine line separates this fear from genuine concern for maintaining high quality and standards and avoiding waste and error.

I suggest some indicators in the form of questions you can ask yourself. Answering "yes" to most of them may lead you to conclude that you indeed need to take measures to address this fear:

1. **Exaggerated reaction to errors:** Do you get frustrated with any inconvenience? Do you lose patience when someone makes a mistake? Do you despair, thinking that things have no solution? Do you tend to see problems as bigger than they are, only to realize that the solution was simpler than you thought? Do you explode first when faced with a problem and solve it later? Do your partners and collaborators feel afraid to tell you when something goes wrong?

2. **Tendency to blame:** Do you always seek to find the person responsible for every mistake or problem and expose them? Do you find it difficult to take responsibility for the problems you face? Do you impose negative consequences for every mistake or inconvenience, no matter how small?

3. **Lack of flexibility:** Do you have trouble accepting that there are different ways of doing things than how you always do them, even if someone else can achieve the same result with a different procedure? Do you stress out when things take unexpected turns?

4. **Difficulty delegating:** Do you always want control over everything to ensure it's done correctly? Do you think that if you don't personally do something, it might go wrong? Do you struggle to allow others to take on responsibilities?

Action Steps to Face and Overcome the Fear of Operational Problems

To confront this fear, we need to develop control mechanisms that allow us to:

1. Minimize the possibility of problems arising.

2. Maximize the possibility of moving forward and overcoming them if we cannot avoid them.

3. Learn to develop assertiveness in communication.

The primary strategy to address the fear of operational problems is detailed planning. This is where we can have the most control. As we plan what we want to do and, above all, design the quality controls we need to ensure that processes are followed, we reduce the likelihood of errors. If we have a sound quality control system, the probability of something going wrong is lower, and less likelihood of failure means less fear.

So, the primary strategy to confront this fear is developing quality systems and controls to maximize monitoring and minimize errors. How can we do this? Here are some strategies that can help you overcome this fear:

1. **Have checklists and quality control lists** that specify all necessary steps and require whoever is executing them to follow them in order, record their execution, and follow up.

2. **Hold regular project status control meetings.** If you have a team of people, internal or external, make sure you have weekly, bi-weekly, or even daily controls, depending on the product or service of your venture. These meetings bring everyone together and ensure everyone is on the same page.

3. **Prepare meeting minutes.** Don't rely solely on memory. Make sure to record, in writing, agreements and commitments, including required completion dates. It doesn't need to be overly bureaucratic; a simple email or message can work. The key is to document and not rely solely on memory for you and the other parties involved.

4. **Automate processes.** The more we automate processes, the more we can reduce the need for human intervention and, consequently, the likelihood of error. As humans, we all make mistakes at some point. No matter how much control we have, there is always a chance of error. Greater automation means that operational failures are less likely to occur.

5. **Use agendas and to-do lists.** Once again, this limits the reliance on our memory (which can sometimes let us down) and forces us to be more organized. I am a fan of to-do lists.

6. **Develop assertive communication:** Through assertiveness, we can maintain emotional control in our relationships and express ourselves in a way that maximizes benefits for all parties involved. Assertiveness is defined as expressing your opinions without aggression and without passivity. It involves respecting others while also respecting what you think. For example, this means being polite to others while being able to say no to situations or proposals that are unsatisfactory, do not lead to achieving your goals, or do not align with your vision.

To communicate assertively, we must achieve emotional control, learn to negotiate, and understand that we don't always win. It involves actively seeking an agreement in which both parties can achieve most of their objectives. Therefore, assertive communication is fundamental to increase success. It's not about winning; it's about achieving mutual benefits.

Assertive attitude is based on self-esteem and self-confidence. To the extent that we believe in ourselves and our project and value our opinions and perceptions, we can defend them and not let them be overshadowed or suppressed. But an assertive attitude also has its foundation in respect for others and tolerance for differences. If we respect others and accept that it's possible to think differently, feel differently, and have different values, we will be able to try to understand their positions. This will help us overcome the fear of damaging our personal relationships due to our entrepreneurial ventures.

These practices and habits can help us safeguard our business operation and make it less vulnerable to failure. They can also give us the confidence not to fear that things can go wrong. How can you maximize the possibility of moving forward and overcoming operational problems if you cannot avoid them? When it's a small operation that depends 100 percent on you, it can fail. When the operation grows, and you need to delegate to your collaborators, it can fail. There is no way to be 100 percent immune. The only way to guarantee that you will never fail is by doing nothing. Our fear of operational problems wants us to freeze. However, if we heed its message, we never progress. Therefore, it is essential to accept the possibility of some failure or problem at some point in the development of our entrepreneurial venture is inevitable.

PART III
FEAR OF INTERNAL CHANGES

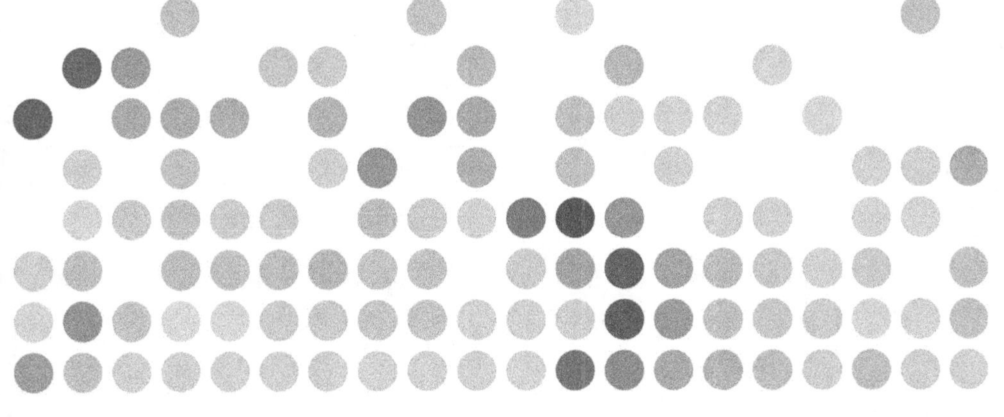

CHAPTER 10
ABOUT FEARS OF INTERNAL CHANGES: FEAR OF FEELING THINGS

"Your fear ends when your mind realizes that it is the one creating that fear."

Alejandro Jodorowsky

We have already reviewed the first part of our wheel of the eight fears of the entrepreneur. Now, we will work with the fears that I have called fears of internal events or fears of "feeling" things. That is, fears caused by things we can feel or think internally, even when they may not necessarily materialize into actual events that occur. Let's think about the fear we felt as children when faced with the need to confess that we broke something at home. The fear of possible punishment or reprimand dominated us, even if sometimes the punishment never came when the moment of action arrived, and our parents understood it was an accident. The fear of the "possible" punishment originated from a reference that, at that moment, existed only in our minds.

Unlike the first four fears we have already analyzed, these next four require us to accept that they relate to situations that come to life in our thoughts and that we can overcome by changing our perception.

According to the model I have developed and propose to you, fears of internal events are less relevant, or at least, they are reported as such by more entrepreneurs, with lower intensity than fears of external events. Fears of internal events account for 43 percent of all the fears reported by entrepreneurs.

Within this broad dimension of fears of internal events or fears of feeling things, I have identified four basic fears that entrepreneurs face:

1. **Fear of feeling incapable:** Fear of not knowing enough about my business sector, not having the knowledge to make appropriate decisions, and being forced to go through unpleasant moments due to my lack of knowledge.

2. **Fear of feeling like a failure:** Fear of realizing that I did not achieve my goals, feeling like a failure, getting depressed, and being emotionally affected. Fear of being unable to carry my business forward and not making good decisions.

3. **Fear of feeling uncomfortable:** Fear of having to make uncomfortable decisions, exposing myself to unpleasant situations, and being forced to do things I don't like or don't feel confident doing.

4. **Fear of being judged:** Fear that family and friends will think it's a bad idea, disapprove of my business, believe I lack the ability to carry it forward, or be disappointed in me.

Fear of Feeling Incapable

In terms of importance, the fear of feeling incapable is the third fear reported by entrepreneurs. It's the third most frequent and the third most intense fear. It represents 13 percent of all internal and external fears and is reported with an average intensity of 36 percent. Let's remember how to interpret this figure: If all entrepreneurs had said they "always" feel all the fears included in this classification, the intensity would have been 100 percent, the maximum possible, indicating that all entrepreneurs always experience all the fears related to feeling incapable. Out of this possible total of absolute fear of feeling incapable, we find 36 percent reported on average.

The fear of feeling incapable primarily includes the fear of not having enough knowledge or not having the necessary and sufficient knowledge or information to make informed decisions. Secondly, it also includes the fear of having to step out of one's comfort zone, defined by what is known and what is mastered or what one has expertise in, and being forced to expose oneself to new situations that challenge current knowledge.

When entrepreneurs report this fear, they indicate that they fear not knowing enough about their business sector, not having the knowledge required to make the right decisions, not having all the information needed for sound decision-making, or not knowing everything necessary to move the business forward.

A common recommendation for entrepreneurs starting a new business is to leverage their existing knowledge base since this increases the chances of success. This means it's more advantageous for us to venture into familiar territory or something more aligned with our interests and knowledge base. However, even if we follow this advice, we will inevitably be exposed to numerous decisions and actions that require knowledge beyond our expertise.

As business owners, we must be involved in every aspect of our company's operations. It doesn't matter if it's a small business where we must handle all tasks or if we choose to seek specialized help in some areas. We still need to have at least a basic knowledge of all areas to select the best collaborator or supplier and to know if the recommendations they provide are in the best interest of our business.

Therefore, the fear of feeling incapable is related to the fear that the knowledge we have at a given moment may not meet the demands of the decisions required for our venture.

Fear of Feeling Like a Failure

The fear of feeling like a failure is the fourth fear reported by entrepreneurs. It's the fourth most frequent and is reported with the same intensity as the fear of feeling incapable. It represents 13 percent of all internal and external fears and has an average intensity of 36 percent.

The fear of feeling like a failure primarily includes the fear of looking in the mirror and recognizing someone who didn't achieve their goals. It's not so much about the fear that the possibility of failure will become a reality but rather the fear of experiencing the set of negative emotions associated with that failure. Let's say it's a fear of anticipating sadness or depression as a result of failure.

When entrepreneurs report this fear, they indicate that they fear the idea that their business might fail, being emotionally affected if things don't go well, feeling like they didn't achieve their goals, or having to start over if things go wrong.

When we experience the fear of failure, we anticipate the discomfort resulting from not achieving our desired goals. The anticipation of the discomfort from failure stops us, sometimes even more than the possibility of failure itself. In other words, we not only fear that things will go wrong, but we also fear that we will "feel like a failure" if things go wrong. The feeling of failure can weigh us down and make it difficult to try something again.

So, the fear of feeling like a failure is related to the fear of experiencing negative feelings and emotional breakdown if things don't go as expected.

Fear of Feeling Uncomfortable

In terms of importance, the fear of feeling uncomfortable is the sixth fear reported by entrepreneurs. It represents 11 percent of all internal and external fears and has an average intensity of 30 percent.

The fear of feeling uncomfortable primarily includes the fear of exposing oneself to unpleasant situations or generating discomfort. In general, it involves being forced to do things one doesn't like or doesn't feel confident doing.

When entrepreneurs report this fear, they indicate that they fear exposing themselves to unpleasant situations, facing moments that make them uncomfortable, making uncomfortable decisions, doing difficult things, or taking on boring and tedious tasks. It's also related in some way to the fear of feeling incapable, as it involves the sensation of discomfort associated with accepting one's lack of knowledge and capability. In this case, more than the incapacity itself, there is a fear that this incapacity will be exposed to others. It manifests in situations where employees or clients ask entrepreneurs something they don't know or in situations where they don't know how to react.

So, the fear of feeling uncomfortable is fundamentally about stepping out of one's comfort zone.

Fear of Being Judged

The fear of being judged is the last fear among entrepreneurs, the least relevant and reported with the lowest intensity. It represents 6 percent of all internal and external fears and has an average intensity of 18 percent.

The fear of being judged includes the fear that family and friends may think their entrepreneurial venture is a bad idea, disapprove of their business, believe they lack the ability to carry it forward, or be disappointed.

When entrepreneurs report this fear, they indicate that they fear their friends may think their venture is crazy or that their family won't approve of their business idea. Ultimately, the fear of being judged implies the fear of not meeting others' expectations of what they can or should achieve.

The fear of being judged is based on a hypothetical situation that is not real yet and may not necessarily happen. Since you haven't acted yet, there is no way for you to be judged or criticized effectively. Consequently, you are scared of something you could potentially feel, but you have no certainty that it will happen. It is based on the expectation that you believe others have of you rather than your expectation of yourself.

The four fears related to internal events are fears of feeling things because of your entrepreneurial activities and exposing yourself to negative emotions such as discomfort, frustration, or rejection.

Just as we did with the fears related to external events, in the following chapters, we will focus on each of the four internal events fears in detail and learn to identify them and, more importantly, successfully overcome them.

CHAPTER 11
FEAR OF FEELING INCAPABLE

*"It's not what you are that holds you back,
it's what you think you are not."*

Denis Waitley

What is and What Does the Fear of Feeling Incapable Entail?

The fear of feeling incapable leads us to believe we are not adequately prepared and lack the knowledge and resources necessary for the project to succeed. In terms of importance, the fear of feeling incapable is the third fear reported by entrepreneurs. It's the third most common and the third most intense fear. It represents 13 percent of all internal and external fears, and it is reported with an average intensity of 36 percent.

When entrepreneurs report this fear, they indicate that they fear not knowing enough about their business sector, not having the knowledge or information necessary to make the right decisions, not having all the information they need to make good decisions, or not knowing everything required to move the business forward. It also includes the fear of having to step out of their comfort zone, defined by what is known and what is mastered, or what they have expertise in, and being forced to expose themselves to new situations that challenge their current knowledge. This fear is related to the psychological phenomenon known as *"Impostor Syndrome,"* a term suggested in 1978 by two clinical psychologists, Pauline Clance and Suzanne Imes.

Impostor Syndrome is defined as the perception that you are not living up to your achievements, that you are not good enough, that you do not deserve your success, and that you have obtained your success by luck or being in the right place and time, not because of your abilities or your dedication, work, and effort. In summary, it represents the fear that at any moment, someone might "unmask" your true self and prove that you are a fraud, an impostor. People who experience this syndrome often attribute their success to external factors, such as luck or deception, rather than acknowledging their own skills and accomplishments. They constantly fear being discovered as "frauds" or "impostors" and are afraid that others will find out they are not as competent as they appear.

Impostor Syndrome is not officially recognized as a mental illness, but it affects many people temporarily or permanently throughout their professional lives. In various sources I reviewed during the research process for this book, I often came across a figure indicating that 70 percent of entrepreneurs and professionals suffer from this syndrome at some point in their lives. I don't usually like to quote statistics if I don't know the source, but it was so consistent across all the documents, always 70 percent, that I decided to share it with you.

Whether it's 70 percent or not, it is clearly something that many entrepreneurs experience. As you read this chapter, you will likely realize that you, too, have suffered from this syndrome at some point.

A common recommendation for an entrepreneur looking to start a new business is to leverage their existing knowledge base, as this increases the chances of success. This means it is more advantageous for us to venture into familiar territory or something that aligns with our interests and knowledge base. However, this is not always the case because sometimes opportunities arise in new areas, and we must study and prepare ourselves. But even if we follow the advice to venture into familiar territory, we will inevitably be exposed to numerous decisions that we must make and actions we must take, which require knowledge beyond our field of expertise.

As business owners, we must get involved with every aspect of our company's operations. It doesn't matter if it's a microbusiness where we must take on all tasks or if we choose to seek specialized help in some areas. Even if we turn to professional help, we still need some knowledge of all areas of our business to select the best collaborator, partner or supplier. It allows us to ensure the decisions they recommend are in the best interest of our business.

So, the fear of feeling incapable is related to the fear that the knowledge we have at a given moment may not meet the demands of the decisions required for our entrepreneurial venture. When we experience this fear, we may feel overwhelmed by the possibility of failure or not living up to the circumstances, which can lead to avoiding certain activities or sabotaging ourselves.

How the Fear of Feeling Incapable Impacts Your Business

For entrepreneurs, the fear of feeling incapable, or Impostor Syndrome, is particularly problematic, as it can stagnate the business. Below, I list some outcomes that can happen in your business because of this fear, all of which undermine the possibility of maximizing your company's success potential:

1. **Conservative and low-risk attitude:** You take fewer risks and become less ambitious in your goals out of fear of failure. To avoid the possibility of failure, you lower your expectations of results to a level where you feel safe. This way, you set a very low bar for what you want to achieve. If you fear feeling incapable, you may avoid situations that involve challenges or are outside your comfort zone, including new jobs, projects, or activities that require learning new skills. The fear of feeling

incapable can lead to avoiding necessary risks for growth and innovation in the business. It can create resistance to changing and exploring new opportunities, limiting the potential for growth and development.

2. **Burnout:** If you fear feeling incapable, you may work much harder than necessary to counteract the possibility of being exposed as a fraud. This leads to extreme exhaustion and fatigue, negatively affecting your business in the long run. You may also demand the same level of extreme effort from your employees, seeking to ensure that the results of your operations are good enough for no one to doubt your ability, convincing yourself that you can do it successfully. These sometimes excessive demands can damage the motivation and commitment of your staff and create a negative organizational culture.

3. **Pursuit of perfectionism:** When faced with the fear of feeling incapable, you become overly critical of yourself and your business and tend to be a perfectionist, which affects the ability to complete goals. The Oxford English Dictionary defines perfectionism as the *"Refusal to accept any standard short of perfection."* Suppose we never dare to finish a project because there is always something we believe can be better. In that case, we negatively affect the efficiency and productivity of the company and are late in responding to our customers.

4. **Inefficient training:** You invest excessive time and resources in courses, training, and education out of fear of not having enough knowledge, but you do not apply this newly acquired knowledge efficiently. Constant study and daily learning are excellent for entrepreneurs. However, you must be careful not to overdo it and become a "professional student," like those who are constantly in courses and training on various topics without taking the time to

use that learning for the benefit of the venture. Training should follow clear objectives and a plan that optimizes its use.

5. **Hypersensitivity to criticism:** You risk becoming very sensitive to the criticism of others, including constructive criticism, for fear of being seen as a failure. This can lead to inconveniences and disagreements with employees, partners, and customers and make you appear arrogant, even extending this negative attribute to the perception of your business.

Signs You Fear Feeling Incapable

How does the fear of feeling incapable and Impostor Syndrome manifest? Various behaviors and reactions on their own may seem common and harmless. Still, they may indicate that you suffer from this fear, which is common among entrepreneurs and can limit the possibilities of success. Once again, I suggest some indicators in the form of questions you can ask yourself. If you find that you answer "yes" to most of them, you should conclude that you need to take steps to address this fear:

1. **Attribution of your success to circumstances and luck (External Locus of Control):** When something goes well, do you tend to say you "got lucky" or that "luck was on your side"? Do you tend to think that the positive things you have achieved in your business result from a set of favorable circumstances and not your work and effort? Do you think that anyone else, in the same circumstances, could have achieved what you have?

2. **Difficulty making decisions:** Do you hesitate a lot when making decisions related to your business because you fear making the wrong decision? Do you try to get many opinions and wait for

many people to agree before deciding on something? Do you change your mind frequently?

3. **Difficulty accepting compliments and recognition:** Do you feel that you don't deserve your success? Do you minimize or underestimate your achievements and downplay their importance? Do you feel uncomfortable when you receive recognition or celebrate an achievement? Do you tend to focus on the negative aspects?

4. **Low self-esteem:** Do you often feel you are not good or valuable enough? Do you constantly compare yourself to others and feel you always fall short? Do you feel insecure about your skills and worry about not measuring up to others? Do you think that other entrepreneurs achieve better results than you with their ventures?

5. **Lack of self-confidence:** Are you afraid that you could be exposed by someone else as a fraud? Do you avoid discussing topics in which you don't feel like an expert? Do you frequently question your abilities, decisions, and actions? Do you have a negative perception of yourself and consider yourself inferior or less capable than others? Do you constantly seek validation from others? Does criticism or rejection deeply affect you?

6. **Excessive self-criticism:** Are you very critical of yourself? Do you tend to focus on your failures and weaknesses? Do you feel less than others, attributing more abilities to others, even if they achieve the same as you? Do you pressure yourself to perform at your best in all areas of your life? Do you never feel satisfied with your achievements and always find faults or areas for improvement?

7. **Procrastination:** Do you postpone tasks or projects until the last moment? Do you avoid doing tasks that you think may not turn out well? Do you make excuses to avoid tackling challenging tasks? Do you easily get distracted by things unrelated to the task you should be doing?

As you can see, most of these behaviors and reactions demonstrate a gap between the actual capabilities you have (as evidenced by your achievements and perceived by others) and the capabilities you attribute to yourself and believe you have, with the latter always being much smaller.

Let's not be confused. Of course, many people and entrepreneurs may be more capable, and there are also businesses with better development than yours. We are not referring to these cases.

When we talk about Impostor Syndrome, we mean the moment when you think you are worse or less qualified, even when the reality of your achievements tells you otherwise.

Impostor Syndrome tends to occur more frequently in high-achieving individuals. They work harder and have high capacity. The problem is not the performance. The problem is the lack of self-perception of merit in that achievement. It is not about cases where the achievement is not reached. It is about cases where it is achieved, but it is not recognized as the result of one's own effort and capacity, and above all, we fear that the lack of capacity we attribute to ourselves may be exposed.

When you face Impostor Syndrome, you want to become the best and work hard for it, but even when you achieve it, it does not alter your distorted perception of the reality of your own capacity.

Action Steps to Face and Overcome the Fear of Feeling Incapable.

Fortunately, Impostor Syndrome is not a personality trait or necessarily permanent. It can be changed and overcome, which is excellent news because the fear of feeling incapable limits entrepreneurs' possibilities for success.

Overcoming the fear of feeling incapable may require personal work on self-exploration and the development of emotional skills. It's important to recognize and challenge negative and self-critical thoughts, set realistic and achievable goals, seek support from trusted individuals, and practice self-reflection and self-acceptance.

We will always have areas of knowledge and skills in which we are lacking. The main strategy to overcome this fear is to carefully analyze the required competencies and determine whether it is true that we have not mastered them.

If, after this analysis, we conclude that we have the required competences, we should take on the challenge.

If, on the contrary, this analysis shows that we indeed lack some necessary skills, it's not the end of the world either. In that case, the next step is to study and reinforce the deficiencies or seek help if they are highly specialized competencies or would take a long time to master. In other words, if you know something, acknowledge it and feel confident. If you don't know it, seek information, study, and better prepare yourself or seek specialized help.

Below, I list some tactics that can help. *However, as in other instances throughout this book, I ask you to keep in mind that, in some more severe or persistent cases, you may require professional assistance through sessions with a qualified psychotherapist if you realize that your fear of incapability or your Impostor Syndrome strongly affects your performance as an entrepreneur. It is important to seek help if this fear interferes with your ability to achieve your goals and enjoy your life. A mental health professional can assist you in building your self-esteem, overcoming perfectionism, and developing skills to tackle challenges.*

1. **Carefully analyze the skills required for success and determine whether you truly master them.** If you do, convince yourself that you are qualified to take on the challenge. If you don't, you must study and reinforce your deficiencies or seek specialized help if it involves highly specific competencies.

2. **Force yourself to accept compliments and recognition.** The next time someone compliments your good work, don't downplay it. Just humbly thank them and accept your achievement.

3. **Avoid perfectionism and accept that mistakes and failures are part of life.** Don't let mistakes drag you down. Correct and learn from them to avoid repeating them, but don't let them hinder or frustrate you. This also involves being resilient. Life, in general, and the life of an entrepreneur even more frequently, presents challenges and unexpected events that disrupt our natural state, alter our plans, and disrupt the expected course of events. When we talk about resilience, we are talking about overcoming these critical moments and adapting to our normal state. Errors and failures are part of life. Instead of seeing them as signs of incompetence, view them as opportunities to grow and improve. Reflect on what you can learn from these experiences and how you can do better in the future.

4. **Avoid comparing yourself to others.** Everyone has their own path. Your achievements are unique, and if they bring you closer to your goal, they are commendable. Focusing on comparisons

takes you away from your own goals and achievements. It distracts you from your personal growth and can lead you to neglect your skills and talents.

5. **List and celebrate your achievements.** Get into the habit of regularly reviewing the goals you have achieved, congratulate yourself, and celebrate whenever you can. When we celebrate something, we take a moment to recognize what we have done. We stop on the path. Instead of looking forward, focusing on the goal, and calibrating how much is left to reach it and what we can do to get there better or faster, we do exactly the opposite. We stop and look back. At that moment, instead of seeing the goal, we focus on the starting line and acknowledge everything we have done to be at this point of our path. No matter how far we must go, we realize we have made progress.

6. **Identify and acknowledge the unique value you and your venture bring to your customers.** Feel proud of that. Communicate it openly.

7. **Take on more controlled risks.** Raise the bar on what you demand from yourself and your venture, and every time you reach a goal, celebrate it and then aspire a little further. Don't rush to pursue difficult goals in opposition to complacency. Take risks but in a controlled environment. Set small, achievable goals that you can work to attain. As you achieve these goals, your self-confidence will gradually strengthen.

8. **Develop more self-confidence.** Ultimately, the fear of feeling incapable and Impostor Syndrome are manifestations of insecurity and low self-confidence. Take the time to understand your strengths, skills, and values. Acknowledge your past achievements and what makes you unique. Accept your areas for improvement and work on them constructively. Seek out people

who encourage, support, and inspire you. Surround yourself with people who believe in you and provide constructive feedback. Social support can play an important role in strengthening your self-confidence.

9. **Cultivate self-compassion.** Learn to treat yourself with respect, kindness, and understanding in moments of difficulty. It doesn't involve self-pity or self-indulgence but rather the acceptance and understanding of your limitations, fostering a positive approach to personal growth.

CHAPTER 12
FEAR OF FEELING LIKE A FAILURE

"It is hard to fail, but it is worse never to have tried to succeed."

Theodore Roosevelt

What Is and What Does the Fear of Feeling Like a Failure Entail?

The fear of feeling like a failure is related to the fear of experiencing negative emotions and emotional breakdown if things don't go as expected. The fear of feeling like a failure primarily includes the fear of looking in the mirror and recognizing someone who didn't achieve their goals. It's not so much about the fear that the possibility of failing will become a reality, but rather the fear of experiencing the set of negative emotions associated with such failure. Let's say it's a fear of anticipating sadness or depression as a result of failure.

The fear of feeling like a failure is the fourth fear reported by entrepreneurs. It's the fourth most common and is presented with the same intensity as the fear of feeling incapable. It represents 13 percent of all internal and external fears and is presented with an average intensity of 36 percent.

When entrepreneurs report this fear, they indicate that they are afraid to think that their business may fail, to be emotionally affected if things don't go well, to feel that they haven't achieved their goals, or to have to start over if things go wrong.

When we experience the fear of feeling like a failure, we anticipate the discomfort involved in not achieving our desired objectives. The anticipation of discomfort from failure stops us, sometimes even more than the possibility of failure itself. In other words, I'm not only afraid that things will go wrong, but I'm afraid that I will "feel like a failure" if things go wrong.

The fear of feeling like a failure, more than the fear of failure itself, can be described as a deep and persistent fear of not reaching personal goals, disappointing oneself or others, and experiencing a sense of incompetence or worthlessness. It is a constant concern about not living up to one's own or others' expectations, which can generate anxiety, stress, and negative self-criticism.

What Is Failure?

Let's start by understanding what failure means. The Oxford English Dictionary (OED) defines *"failure"* as *"The fact of failing to effect one's purpose; want of success; an instance of this"* and defines *"fail"* as *"To be unsuccessful in an attempt or enterprise."* This means an adverse result of an enterprise or business unfavorable or contrary to what was expected. However, we are talking about the fear of "feeling like a failure" and not just the fear of "failure" itself. In essence, our fear extends beyond the anticipation of things going awry; it encompasses the dread of the potential negative emotional impact it may inflict upon us.

The feeling of failure can be demoralizing and hinder your willingness to try again. Consequently, feeling like a failure implies *"feeling discredited due to the failures suffered in one's attempts or aspirations."* As we don't want to feel discredited in front of others, we develop an irrational and persistent fear of making mistakes in front of others.

The fear of failure has several aspects:

1. **Objective:** Related to facts: The fear of not reaching the goal (failing).

2. **Subjective:** Related to your inner world: The fear of feeling bad for not reaching the goal (feeling like a failure).

3. **Social:** Related to how others see us: The fear that others will discredit us for not reaching the goal (being seen as a failure).

The fear of feeling like a failure is associated with a fatalistic view of failure. When we, as entrepreneurs, feel this fear, we often associate it with a shameful, frustrating, and unacceptable situation, and we tend to see the world in extremes, in black and white. We fail to realize that viewing failure as a learning experience is possible. We don't understand that it's possible to see failure as something that, yes, is an obstacle in achieving the goal but also as something that is surmountable. The catastrophic view of failure can be generated by cultural, social, and family behaviors in which success is highly valued, and failure is heavily punished. We learn to magnify the negative effects of failure, imagining that it will have a devastating impact on our personal, professional, and, consequently, entrepreneurial life.

How the Fear of Feeling Like a Failure Impacts Your Business

The fear of feeling like failure is often related to high personal or social expectations, perfectionism, and excessive self-demand. A person may have a distorted view of success and fear that any outcome that doesn't meet those expectations will be considered a failure. This fear can be paralyzing and limit the willingness to take risks, face new challenges, or pursue meaningful goals.

Some of the negative consequences that this fear can bring to your business include the following:

1. **Self-sabotage:** One of the main negative consequences of this fear is that it undermines the entrepreneur's and the business's goals. Self-sabotage is a form of self-destructive behavior in which a person consciously or unconsciously sabotages their efforts and opportunities due to a fear of failure. This involves abandoning goals considered difficult or where one feels the likelihood of success is low. Excuses are sought to justify the abandonment of goals with rational explanations so as not to feel bad about not trying. As a result of this self-sabotage, one may also avoid relationships or collaborations that could be beneficial to the business. The entrepreneur may fear the possibility of rejection, judgment, or not meeting the expectations of others.

2. **Avoiding taking risks:** Related to the self-sabotage we just described the fear of feeling like a failure can make entrepreneurs avoid taking some risks necessary for business success. They may choose to stay in their comfort zone and avoid any situation where they might face the possibility of failure. And the thing is, when risks are not taken, even if they are controlled risks, it's very difficult to achieve growth and innovation in the business.

3. **Stagnation and lack of growth:** The fear of feeling like a failure can lead to a static mindset rather than a growth mindset. You may settle for the current state of the business and avoid taking steps to expand its reach or improve. This can limit the growth potential and leave the business lagging behind the competition.

4. **Resistance to change:** The fear of feeling like a failure can make entrepreneurs resistant to making necessary changes in the business. They may fear that such changes will lead to failure and prefer to keep things as they are. However, a lack of adaptability

and flexibility can hinder the business's ability to stay relevant and competitive in an ever-evolving environment. The possibility of innovation, essential for business success, requires having an open mindset towards change. When there is a fear of feeling like a failure, and consequently, changes are avoided, the business is increasingly moving away from the path of modernization and the possibilities of standing out in its sector.

Signs You Fear Feeling Like a Failure

This fear can manifest in various ways, such as the fear of making mistakes, the fear of rejection or disapproval, the fear of not meeting established goals, or the fear of losing social status or others' approval. The person may feel intense internal pressure to achieve success and avoid any situation that may lead to a perception of failure. Below are some indicators in the form of questions you can ask yourself, and if you find that you answer "yes" to most of them, you should conclude that you need to take steps to address this fear:

1. **Tendency to avoid challenges:** Do you avoid taking risks or facing new challenges due to the fear of not meeting expectations or making mistakes? Do you frequently reject new ideas, even with excuses you consider rational and logical? Have you found yourself discarding goals that initially seemed attractive but later appeared too difficult or unattainable?

2. **Constant procrastination:** Do you tend to postpone important tasks out of fear of not achieving desired results or failing? Do you avoid making decisions about which you're not certain to succeed? Do you currently have several pending decisions that you should have made a long time ago, but you're hesitating because you don't want to make mistakes?

3. **Excessive self-criticism:** Are you very hard on yourself? Do you constantly criticize and negatively judge yourself when you don't meet your goals or expectations? Do you become emotionally distraught when you fail to achieve an objective? Do you often tell yourself that you're a failure and someone who hasn't achieved anything in life? Do you downplay your accomplishments?

4. **Feeling of stagnation:** Do you feel like you've become stagnant in your life or entrepreneurship due to the fear of failure and not achieving your goals? Would you like to reach new goals but find yourself stuck without knowing how to set them? Do you have difficulty visualizing the future you want for your business? Is it challenging to chart the path you want to take to lead your business to success? Do you feel like you're at a crossroads and don't know how to move forward?

5. **Feeling of discomfort and anxiety:** Do you experience anxiety, stress, or significant emotional distress when you face situations where there's a possibility of failure? Are you greatly concerned about the possibility of your business failing? Does the possibility of looking in the mirror and recognizing someone who didn't achieve their goals give you anxiety? Do you easily become sad or depressed when things don't go as planned or desired? Do you struggle to start over after something has gone wrong?

Action Steps to Face and Overcome the Fear of Feeling Like a Failure

I acknowledge that I am a bit of an outlier when it comes to statistics. While most of my colleagues in psychology, management, and entrepreneurship dislike statistics, I've always enjoyed them and find them a wonderful resource for decision-making. Anything related to probabilities is a topic that often intimidates and repels people within the field of statistics. If you've ever had to study statistics, you might relate to this feeling (or maybe not). However, probability theory includes clear, powerful, and highly useful concepts for our daily lives. It's also an excellent tool for explaining the logic behind overcoming the fear of feeling like a failure.

Let's try to simplify it to better understand how a statistical concept can help us reduce this fear. We'll consider the goal we're trying to achieve with the decision we need to make as an "event."

According to probability theory, each "event" has a probability of success and a probability of failure. In any decision to achieve our goal, we continually expose ourselves to the probability of achieving the objective (success) and not achieving it (failure).

The fear of the probability of failing has two possible causes:

1. We don't know the probabilities of success and failure.

2. The probability of failure is very high.

Therefore, the best way to reduce the fear of feeling like a failure is to reduce the probability of failing and increase the probability of success. The probabilities of success and failure always add up to 100 percent. The more you increase one, the more you automatically reduce the other.

It's as simple as that.

So, the primary task to reduce this fear is to do everything within your power to increase the probability of success. Automatically, the probability of failure will be diminished. With a higher probability of success, there's less risk in making the decision and, therefore, less fear of making a mistake.

Strategy #1 for reducing your fear of feeling like a failure: **Increase the probability of success** so that the fear of failure is lessened.

How can you increase the probability of success? Basically, by working on rigorous planning and reducing levels of uncertainty. Planning and information are the two keywords and activities.

1. **Plan rigorously.** Leave as little as possible to chance and place as much as possible under your control. The better you understand what will happen because of your decisions and the more control you have over the outcomes, the more you avoid improvisation, uncertainty, and surprises due to unforeseen events.

2. **Set intermediate goals that lead you to the final goal and that you can achieve progressively.** This way, you can adjust if necessary and increase the probability of reaching the objective. Instead of setting a very complex final goal, work on establishing successive approaches to the goal. Each advancement will be a small success and will progressively work to bring you closer to the desired success. In addition to reducing uncertainty, this also increases your motivation and sense of achievement. Both elements contribute to reducing your fear of feeling like a failure.

3. **Create a scenario analysis and decision tree.** Analyze all possible things that can happen and prepare plans for each scenario. Evaluate the best scenario with the best chance of achieving the objective. Let's call this scenario "A." But don't just work on plan A. Prepare a plan B, and if necessary, a plan C, or as many as needed.

The better you plan and the more information you try to obtain about the situation while analyzing the options, the more you reduce levels of uncertainty and, consequently, increase the probability of achieving success. And when you manage to increase the chances of success, what happens? Indeed, the probability of failure automatically decreases. And if the probability of failing is lower, your fear of failure is also lower.

Strategy #2 for reducing your fear of feeling like a failure: **Be prepared for the possibility of failure.** If it doesn't catch you off guard, you'll feel less fear (as in the popular saying, *"A warned war doesn't kill soldiers"*).

In your scenario analysis, never forget to consider the worst-case scenario. What's the worst that could happen if you fail? What are the possible negative consequences for your business if you don't achieve the objective? Then, always work on a plan (C, D, or Z, however you like to call it) to deal with this worst-case scenario.

Work to succeed but prepare for failure. In this way, in addition to increasing the chances of achieving your goal (success), you know in advance how to act if the event of failure occurs. Even if the probability of failure is low because you've done your homework and prepared an excellent and detailed plan, you can still face all contingencies. Prepare for failure, even if you plan to succeed. That way, the possibility of failure won't catch you by surprise, and your fear of failing will be much lower.

Strategy #3 for reducing your fear of feeling like a failure: **Eliminate the drama and negative connotations of failure.** Accept that it's not the end of the world and that it happens to everyone at some point.

Change the negative connotations of the concept of failure. While failure will always be defined as an *"adverse, unfavorable, or contrary to what was expected"* outcome, focus only on the fact that it is "contrary" to what was expected (you didn't achieve success) and eliminate from your mind the negative connotations of being "adverse" and "unfavorable."

Change the negative connotation of failure by associating it with learning instead. This way, you will fear failure less and less. You must understand that failure in some projects is a part of life and happens to everyone at some point or another.

No one has been successful all the time. No one can say they've never failed.

So, reframe failure. Stop seeing failure as the end of the world and start seeing it as an experience that allows you to learn and grow. Failure is necessary and teaches us lessons. We learn from each fall. Failure is part of life, and it's inevitable. It will show up sometime. You can only work to reduce its likelihood and prevent it from happening frequently. But you can never reduce the probability of failure to zero in all your decisions.

Don't avoid the possibility of failure. When you run from failure, you're leaving aside the possibility of success.

Change your concept of feeling like a failure and **start accepting that being a failure is someone who doesn't try,** as Theodore Roosevelt's quote at the beginning of this chapter suggests. Think about how much worse you'll feel when you regret never having tried.

A popular saying (whose author I don't know) goes: *"Failure is a wrong path to the goal."* It's a very positive view of failure. This saying suggests that you need to correct your course to get back on the right track.

Accept the reality that nobody is perfect. Eliminate the drama of the failure situation, and don't run away from the possibility of failure. Face it with planning and preparation tools. With these strategies, you will succeed in reducing the fear of feeling like a failure.

CHAPTER 13
FEAR OF FEELING UNCOMFORTABLE

"Insanity is doing the same thing over and over again and expecting different results."

Albert Einstein

What Is and What Does the Fear of Feeling Uncomfortable Entail?

The fear of feeling uncomfortable is primarily related to the fear of leaving our comfort zone. Leaving the comfort zone refers to the idea of facing and overcoming new, challenging, or unknown situations. It involves stepping out of comfort and routine and entering territories that require effort, personal growth, and pushing our limits.

The fear of feeling uncomfortable is the sixth most significant fear reported by entrepreneurs. It represents 11 percent of all internal and external fears and is typically experienced with an average intensity of 30 percent.

This fear primarily includes the fear of exposing oneself to unpleasant or uncomfortable situations, such as engaging in activities one dislikes or feels insecure about. It generally involves being forced to do things that one finds uncomfortable or challenging. It is also somewhat related to the fear of feeling incapable, as it encompasses the discomfort associated with acknowledging one's lack of knowledge and ability. In this case, more than the inability itself, there is a fear that this incapability will be exposed to others. This fear can manifest when employees or clients ask questions one doesn't know the answers to or when faced with situations where one doesn't know how to react.

What is comfort for an entrepreneur? Routines, doing things well, what we know and handle with ease—these things bring us comfort. They require less effort, and we understand the possible outcomes, which are usually satisfying. Our comfort zone includes aspects of life where we have control because we are in familiar territory. It's a space we dominate that is familiar and doesn't surprise us. We feel so good in our comfort zone that the fear of discomfort paralyzes us, and as a result, it hinders the progress of our entrepreneurship.

Being in a comfort zone is good because it provides pleasant sensations and security. However, if we always live in this zone, we risk never changing, growing, learning, or experiencing new things. We close ourselves off to new opportunities.

If we want to progress with our entrepreneurship, we must step out of our comfort zone and overcome the fear of discomfort. We must recognize that if we want different results, we must leave behind routines and change our usual way of doing things, as suggested by Albert Einstein's quote at the beginning of this chapter. Leaving our comfort zone means facing the unknown. It means potential dangers. The consequences we anticipate may be unpleasant.

Humans are wired to stay in their comfort zones and seek security. The prospect of discomfort due to a lack of control scares us. We fear losing or risking what we know we have with certainty.

In this case, fear arises from anticipating potential discomfort, not from actual discomfort. It leads us to avoid potential discomfort (which hasn't occurred yet, but we assume it will). Once again, we're talking about the fear of "feeling" things: fear arises from anticipating discomfort rather than the discomfort itself. We believe it's possible to feel bad when leaving our comfort zone, and as a result, fear constrains us.

A model proposed by Matti Hemmi of Inknowation (2012) suggests three concentric zones. At the core is the comfort zone, small and sheltered. Surrounding the comfort zone are more interesting and growth-oriented zones. When you venture into these zones, you can spread your wings and grow in life and entrepreneurship.

The **comfort zone** is where you feel secure and seek refuge in the known. It's the core of the model. It encompasses everything you know, what you like, what you understand, and what doesn't surprise you. In short, the comfort zone is everything within your control.

Around the comfort zone is the **learning zone**. Think of a larger concentric circle that surrounds the core comfort zone. You enter this learning zone when you venture out of your small comfort zone and explore new directions and experiences. It's a zone of uncertainty and unfamiliarity. This second zone allows you to grow and expand the comfort zone's boundaries to new limits. It's an area where we allow ourselves to discover new things and experiences. We don't know the consequences, but we're willing to trade comfort for learning. However, it's a zone where we feel less in control because it's more uncertain and filled with new concepts, behaviors, and ideas.

Beyond the learning zone is where the fear of discomfort truly takes place. Imagine a third concentric circle around the learning zone, even larger. This zone is known as the **panic zone**. It's an unknown territory that generates anxiety because it has the potential to create discomfort. In this zone, paralysis or "inaction" often occurs due to fear. However, this zone has the potential to change from a panic zone to a **magical zone** of growth. This is where great challenges lie. It's the area where entrepreneurs should feel the most freedom to explore, develop, and grow.

When we overcome the fear of discomfort generated by the panic zone, we can transform it into a magical zone. When we change the panic zone into a magical zone, we gain control over our fear of discomfort and welcome new experiences and the risks they entail. We achieve this when we understand that to reach new goals and develop our business, we must dare to take risks and behave differently. We must expand our horizons, open our wings, and explore the world beyond what we know and where we feel safe.

How the Fear of Feeling Uncomfortable Impacts Your Business

As entrepreneurs, living constantly within our comfort zone is detrimental because it stagnates our projects and businesses. We become entrepreneurs who don't seem like entrepreneurs, with strict and monotonous daily routines and controlled risk levels. This is contrary to what defines us as entrepreneurs.

Some of the negative consequences that this fear can bring to your business include the following:

1. **Stagnation:** If an entrepreneur, and consequently their company, is unwilling to leave their comfort zone, they will likely stagnate. The lack of initiative to seek new opportunities or face challenges can result in a loss of competitiveness in the market. As we saw in the model explained earlier, you remain confined to that core if you don't expand your comfort zone by stepping outside of it. You never enter the learning zone. And without learning, there is no progress or evolution. The first thing that happens when you're afraid to move away from your comfort zone is that you come to a standstill with no chance of moving forward.

2. **Lack of innovation:** When we don't take the risk of venturing beyond the known and exploring that learning zone, we end up constantly repeating behavior and thought patterns that we have used before and that have proven to work well. As a result, we don't innovate. An entrepreneurial venture open to innovation has a better chance of achieving success, differentiation, and growth, impacting its consumers. Conversely, entrepreneurship that is not open to innovation, instead of being the point of reference where others turn for information, becomes a follower, trying to figure out what its competition has done to replicate it.

3. **Conformity:** The fear of discomfort can foster a culture of conformity within the company. A conformist entrepreneur may be content with the current state of their business and not actively seek new growth opportunities. They may settle for the current situation and avoid taking risks or exploring new ideas. And this attitude permeates the entire organization. Employees will also avoid challenging the status quo, expressing new ideas, or questioning existing practices. This mindset limits creativity and critical thinking and can lead to a lack of organizational improvement and growth.

4. **Resistance to organizational change:** If leaders and employees in a company fear discomfort, they are likely to resist organizational changes, such as restructuring, implementing new technologies, or adopting new strategies. This resistance can hinder the company's ability to adapt and improve efficiency.

Signs You Fear Feeling Uncomfortable

Recognizing that you have a fear of stepping out of your comfort zone is the first step in overcoming it. Below are some signs that could indicate you have a fear of leaving your comfort zone. Just like with the other fears we've discussed I'll present these indicators as questions you can ask yourself. If you realize that you answer "yes" to most of them, you should conclude that you need to take steps to address this fear:

1. **Comfort in routine:** Do you feel extremely comfortable in your daily routine and avoid any situation that disrupts it? Do you prefer to maintain familiarity and predictability? Do you get easily upset when someone or something forces you to deviate from your daily routine and do things differently from what you have planned? Is your daily routine flexible?

2. **Regular avoidance of new or unknown situations:** Do you find it challenging to attend work meetings where you don't know anyone? Do you avoid trying new activities? Does it bother you when the applications and systems you use undergo updates that require you to change procedures that you're accustomed to? Is it difficult for you to accept cultural differences you observe in other countries or business environments where you need to develop relationships? Does it bother you to change work systems?

3. **Difficulty in negotiations and sales:** Do you avoid participating in these interactions due to fear of facing objections, rejections, or uncomfortable situations during the deal-closing process? Do you avoid conflict, even if you are in the right? Are you willing to sacrifice benefits in a negotiation to avoid an uncomfortable conversation with a client?

4. **Anticipatory anxiety:** Before facing a situation that you believe could make you feel uncomfortable, do you experience physical symptoms such as excessive sweating, heart palpitations, trembling, or stomach pain? Does confronting a situation you know will be uncomfortable keep you up at night?

5. **Delegation of tasks not based on who will do it better, but solely because they are things you don't like to do:** Do you delegate tasks only because you don't like doing them or feel uncomfortable, even though the person you delegate them to may not be able to perform them as well as you can? Do you "pass the buck" to partners or collaborators when making tough decisions?

Action Steps to Face and Overcome the Fear of Feeling Uncomfortable

The most difficult step is deciding to do it. The fear of discomfort that paralyzes the progress of your entrepreneurship is an anticipation of discomfort that hasn't occurred. We often think there's a possibility of feeling uncomfortable or of things not going well or being unpleasant. However, many times, the uncomfortable consequences we anticipate aren't as bad as we think, or they don't happen at all.

1. **Face the fear head-on: Confront it.** Face that anxiety that change causes. Once you overcome that initial confrontation, everything might turn out easier than you expected. It's the decision that leads us to accept injections, even if we fear the pain; to jump into cold water, even if we think it'll be uncomfortable; to call that person we like and ask them out, even if they might say no. In all these cases, if you reflect on your past everyday experiences, you'll likely find that the injection didn't hurt as much, and if it

did, it was only for a short time; that once you were in the water and your body adapted to the temperature, you actually enjoyed the experience; and that in many instances, the person you liked accepted your invitation, leading to enriching and lasting relationships.

The call that was so hard for you to make to a potential client seemed more difficult before you made it, but once you picked up the phone and exchanged the first words. it was easy. That presentation you had to give in public was tough when you stood in front of the group, but once you started speaking on the topic, you felt right at home. Those first days learning to use a new system were tedious and slow, but once you mastered those processes, you realized that you had solved problems and were working more efficiently.

That first step, the hardest one, is simultaneously the most relieving. It's a crucial moment, but it's just that—a moment. Once you're on the other side of that fear, the satisfaction of having faced it and realizing that the discomfort was larger in your mind truly brings pleasure and builds your confidence. That's when you start seeing the benefits of change and enjoy learning and moving into that magical zone.

2. **Build self-confidence:** As discussed in previous chapters, a fundamental element in overcoming fear is increasing self-confidence and self-esteem. Believe in yourself and what you're capable of. As you work on your self-confidence, it will become easier to take that first step to leave your comfort zone. That's why the learning zone is so important. As you learn, you expand your comfort zone and progressively approach changes and innovations with greater confidence.

3. **Be prepared for new experiences:** When you decide to step out of your comfort zone, it's important to be adequately prepared to increase your chances of reaching that magical zone. Look within your comfort zone for available resources. Everything you've mastered has helped you achieve what you have. Leverage that knowledge to confront the learning and panic zones.

4. **Don't leave your comfort zone to improvise:** Just because you don't know for certain what lies beyond doesn't mean you can't have a plan. To the extent that you have a plan and a strategy, even including alternative plans to address possible failures in the original plan, you'll have many more opportunities to overcome the fear of discomfort. You'll start moving into the magical zone where progress and success can develop.

5. **Try doing things with fear:** Start with small things that involve manageable discomfort and have a low likelihood of catastrophic consequences. Force yourself to regularly step out of your comfort zone with small, inconsequential challenges. Try new dishes at your favorite restaurant instead of ordering the same dish you always love, change brands of products, or just try different activities on weekends—anything that personally involves a small challenge to your routines and comfort. Gradually increase the levels of risk and apply the same technique to matters related to your professional life and entrepreneurship. You will progressively become more open to taking greater risks without fearing discomfort.

For organizations to thrive in a changing business environment, it's essential they overcome this fear, foster a culture of openness to change, and encourage the constant pursuit of new opportunities.

CHAPTER 14
FEAR OF BEING JUDGED

*"Don't let the noise of others' opinions
drown out your own inner voice."*

Steve Jobs

What Is and What Does the Fear of Being Judged Entail?

The fear of entrepreneurs being judged by others is the last of the fears we define as the fear of internal changes—in other words, the fear of "feeling" things. In this case, it's the fear of feeling questioned, disapproved of, or rejected because of the decisions we make with our entrepreneurship.

The fear of being judged is the fear that appears last among entrepreneurs. It's the least relevant and is experienced with the lowest intensity. It represents 6 percent of all internal and external fears and is typically experienced with an average intensity of 18 percent.

This fear is a consequence of the human needing to be accepted and fit into our reference social groups. The fear of being judged includes the fear that family and friends might think our entrepreneurship is a bad idea, disapprove of our business, believe we lack the capability to carry it forward, or even the fear that we might disappoint them.

When entrepreneurs report this fear, they indicate that they are afraid that their friends might think their entrepreneurship is crazy or that their family disapproves of their business idea. They fear their friends or acquaintances might think their idea is a flawed business, a worthless idea to pursue. Ultimately, the fear of being judged implies the fear of not meeting the expectations others have of what we can or should achieve. It even includes the fear of disappointing the expectations that we "believe" others have of us. Sometimes, this fear of being judged is so unfounded that it's possible that our friends or family don't think of us and our entrepreneurship in the way we imagine.

The fear of being judged is based on a hypothetical situation, something that is not yet real and may not necessarily happen. Since you haven't acted yet, there is no way for others to judge or criticize you. Consequently, you fear something you could potentially feel, but you are not certain it will happen. It is based on the expectation that you think others have of you rather than your expectation of yourself.

We are social beings by nature. The Learned Motivations Theory proposed by American psychologist David McClelland in 1961 highlights three basic motivations in every human being: the need for achievement, the need for affiliation, and the need for power. According to McClelland's theory, the need for affiliation involves belonging to a group, feeling part of one's environment, and being accepted. People with a high need for affiliation seek social approval, seek the company of others, and seek acceptance in social groups. They desire to be accepted, loved, and valued by others.

The fear of being judged is the counterpart of this basic need for affiliation and reflects the fear of not being accepted or fitting in properly with your environment. When our need for affiliation is strong, the fear of not being accepted or fitting into our environment increases. When we behave driven by this high need for affiliation and motivated by a heightened fear of being judged, we tend to seek to please others and make decisions based on what others consider appropriate rather than being guided by our convictions.

The fear of being judged originates from childhood throughout our upbringing. As children, we tend to seek approval from our parents and teachers. As we grow, we seek approval from our peer groups, our friends. When entering professional life, we seek approval from colleagues, bosses, clients, and collaborators. If, during that formative process, we learned that being ourselves could lead to rejection, we will more likely disguise our true selves to appear better to others. Therefore, this fear of judgment can stem from previous experiences of criticism or social rejection. People who have experienced rejection may be more sensitive to the possibility of being judged and, as a result, may avoid social situations or suppress their authentic opinions and behaviors to avoid rejection.

The fear of being judged, when developed from childhood, makes us avoid showing who we truly are. We prefer to adopt behaviors, beliefs, and values that we think others like more and will motivate them to accept us better.

As a psychological concept, the fear of being judged is conceptualized as Fear of Negative Evaluation (FNE). Some studies have developed scales to measure this fear. These instruments assess the intensity and characteristics of the fear that a person experiences when facing the possibility of being judged or evaluated negatively by others. Among them, we can mention the Fear of Negative Evaluation Scale (FNE), developed by Watson and Friend in 1969, and the Brief Fear of Negative Evaluation Scale (BFNE), an abbreviated version of the FNE scale developed by Leary in 1983.

In its most extreme and irrational form, the fear of being judged becomes what is known as *"social anxiety"* or *"social phobia." Of course, this is a case that would already require the assistance of a specialized professional. Today, we do not want to focus on the extremes but rather on the normal and common fear that someone might think what we are doing and our decisions are incorrect and consequently discredit us. Once again, I remind you that if you understand that your fear of being judged and the social anxiety you experience are extreme or cannot be*

How Fear of Being Judged Impacts Your Business

The fear of being judged hinders and delays us on the path to achieving our dreams and goals. The fear of being judged manifests in various ways. It's the fear of the infamous "what will they say," the fear of making a fool of ourselves, the fear of disappointing others. In all these cases, it's the fear of exposing ourselves to others' opinions.

1. **Poor execution:** We fear that others might criticize our actions or decisions, creating a negative, vicious circle. Since we fear exposing ourselves to criticism, this fear affects our execution, and what could go well under normal conditions becomes more likely to go wrong because we are nervous and anxious. As things go wrong (or "less well" than expected), we do not receive approval, and our initial fear of criticism is reinforced.

   Imagine, for example, a situation where you must make an important presentation to a client about your project. Even though you have prepared very well and have a perfect understanding of the topic, you are afraid the client may not accept your idea. This fear generates anxiety, and when facing your client, anxiety prevents you from giving your best. Consequently, your presentation is not as good as it could have been, and you fail to make the right impression on your client, causing them to reject your idea or make judgments and criticisms about your project. As you can see, the fear of rejection affects your behavior, your suboptimal behavior affects the outcome, and the low-quality result generates criticism and rejection, reinforcing your initial fear. Like any vicious circle, the way to end it is to break it at some point, so it does not continue to feed itself. You must break the circle at the point you can control, and that point is your fear of being judged. If you control your fear of being judged, you disrupt the vicious circle.

2. **Sacrifice of personal vision and goals:** When we fear being judged by others or disappointing them, we may sacrifice our dreams. We may try to adjust our goals and the vision we seek for our business to what others give us as a reference for what is acceptable or socially expected to succeed. In this way, we hold back our dreams, our real passions, and conform to others' expectations. Don't get me wrong; it's not bad to listen to advice, but it's not advisable to conform to others' opinions by sacrificing what you believe in or want to achieve.

3. **Inconsistency in the vision:** If you fear being judged by others and try to adjust your business goals to please as many reference points as possible, you will likely end up with a blurry, changing, and inconsistent vision of your business. When you have a clear vision, it's YOUR vision. You can (and should) share it with various groups related to your business (partners, collaborators, clients, suppliers) and your personal life (family and friends). You can also adjust and enrich it based on valuable mentorship and conversations with any of these people. What you should never do is change it every time someone questions a decision or thinks your vision is inadequate. You must believe in your project enough to develop and maintain a clear vision. And you must be the one to convey it to your associates (not the other way around).

4. **Changing decisions:** When you try to please and be on good terms with everyone, your business is affected because you end up making decisions that can be contradictory and changing instead of following a clear plan and vision.

Signs You Fear Being Judged

The fear of being judged by others can manifest in various ways, both physically and emotionally. Once again, as in the previous chapters, I'll share some signs that could indicate you fear being judged, along with some indicators in the form of questions you can ask yourself. If you find that you answer "yes" to most of them, you should conclude that you need to take steps to address this fear:

1. **Excessive concern about appearance:** Do you worry excessively about your physical appearance? Do you spend a lot of time and money on makeup, clothing, and accessories to appear more attractive or acceptable in the eyes of others? Does it bother you if your physical appearance is not suitable for representing your business or could potentially cause rejection among your clients? Do you dress for your clients more than for yourself?

2. **Indecisiveness:** Do you postpone important decisions until you can talk to all the people you think may have a relevant opinion? Do you frequently change decisions you've made after receiving opposing comments or suggestions to change them? Do you struggle to decide when you're not sure if that decision will be well-received by others? Do you decide against your own belief solely because someone you consider an expert advised you to choose differently?

3. **Self-censorship and lack of authenticity:** Do you find yourself suppressing your authentic opinions, emotions, or behaviors out of fear of being judged? Do you worry more about fitting into others' expectations than being true to yourself? Do you prefer to adapt to the styles and needs of your reference group rather than acting according to what you really want to do? Do you feel uncomfortable expressing your opinions or ideas?

4. **Constant need for approval:** Do you heavily rely on the approval of others to feel valuable? Do you constantly seek external validation and avoid making decisions based on your own values and desires? Do you often catch yourself waiting for specific individuals to make positive comments about you, your entrepreneurship, or your work? Do you depend on external opinions and approval to feel good about yourself?

5. **Excessive sensitivity to criticism:** Does any criticism or negative comment deeply affect you, even if it's constructive? When someone criticizes a decision you've made, do you feel personally attacked? Do you fear that others will see you as inadequate or insufficient? Do you go to great lengths to avoid decisions that could expose you to public criticism?

6. **Social anxiety:** Do you often feel nervous or anxious in social situations and constantly worry about how others perceive you? Do you avoid social situations or events where you feel vulnerable or exposed?

7. **Low self-esteem:** Do you sometimes feel like you're not good enough or don't meet others' expectations? Do you tend to constantly compare yourself to others and feel inferior? Do you struggle to accept compliments?

Action Steps to Face and Overcome the Fear of Being Judged

The fear of being judged is generally based on a hypothetical situation, something that is not real yet and may not necessarily happen. Since you haven't acted, there's no way for others to judge or criticize you. Consequently, you are afraid of something you might potentially feel, but you're not certain it will happen.

And that's excellent news. Because your fear is based on something that hasn't occurred, it is possible to control and change it. Here are some strategies you can use to control your fear of being judged when you realize that it's the cause of your indecision to act:

1. **Know yourself:** Understand your strengths and weaknesses. When you know what you are or are not capable of, it becomes more difficult for others to easily convince you that you are incapable or likely to fail. Don't be afraid to acknowledge your strengths or think that you might be perceived as arrogant. If you're good at something, accept it with pride and stand up for your expertise and abilities. Also, don't hesitate to discover and accept your weaknesses or areas of opportunity. Knowing them is the foundation that will allow you to make the right decisions to correct and improve.

2. **Build self-esteem and self-confidence:** Value yourself for who you are. Be authentic. Being authentic is more valuable than pleasing others, so it's important that you feel comfortable with yourself and know your worth. Above all, understand that your self-worth doesn't depend on what others think of you. *If you find overcoming self-esteem issues difficult, seek help from a specialized therapist who can assist you with suitable strategies.*

3. **Trust your intuition and passions:** Dare to say "yes" to your intuition and what your inner self, heart, and reasoning tell you is the right path. Don't sacrifice your beliefs, values, and what you think is right to please others. Other people's paths are just that. Dare to walk your own, which is unique and irreplaceable.

4. **Invest in yourself:** Study and seek continuous improvement. This will make you feel increasingly confident about your abilities and skills and make it easier to accept your authority to defend your views and decisions. Entrepreneurs must study every day and

strive to excel in various areas. Read constantly, enroll in training programs, attend conferences and professional development events in your business sector.

5. **Silence your inner critic:** Often, it's you who sabotages your own efforts. Before others criticize, mock, or discourage you, you've already done it to yourself. When that inner critical voice questions your plans and what you know you can achieve, learn to silence it. Don't self-destruct.

6. **Accept that there will always be critics, no matter what you do: Let them talk.** No matter how much effort we make, none of us will always please and satisfy everyone else. There's no way to please everyone. It's a reality, and we must accept it.

7. **Prevent what others think of you from affecting you emotionally:** Accept criticism and learn to treat it appropriately. Sometimes, the judgments of others open your eyes and help you improve. Other times, they only harm you. The better you know yourself, the easier it will be to differentiate between the two.

8. **Try not to let what others think of you become the guide for your decisions:** Learn to make decisions based on your judgment. If you seek advice or are exposed to others, consider all comments and suggestions that seem appropriate to you. However, refrain from making decisions solely based on someone else's judgment unless it aligns with your criteria or you are convinced it offers a better or more valid perspective.

9. **Stop judging others:** Even if we think we don't, we constantly judge those around us, from critiquing their way of speaking to their personal style and business decisions. I'm sure that if you pay close attention to your behavior, you can identify daily moments when, even without ill intentions, you tend to pass judgment on

others without being asked for it. Every time you catch yourself passing judgment on someone else, stop and suspend that activity. Over time, as you judge others less and less, you will gradually feel less apprehensive about the possibility that others might do the same to you.

PART IV
WORKING ON OUR FEARS:
THE TOOLBOX

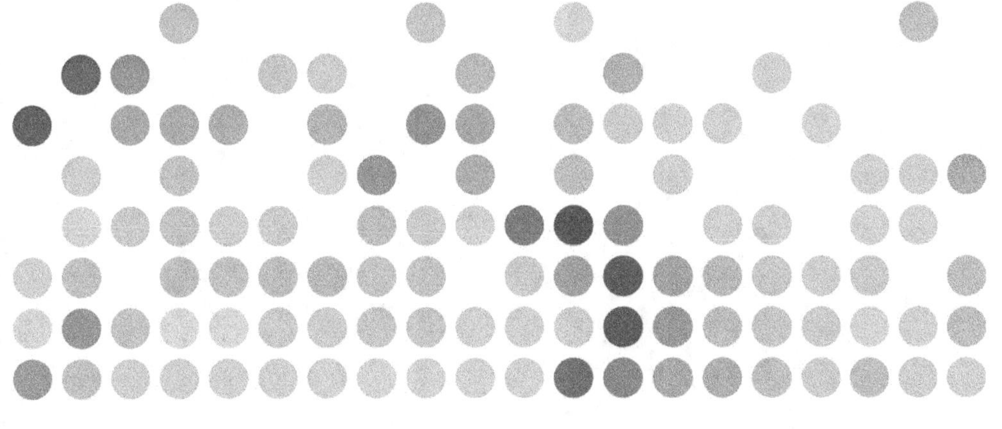

CHAPTER 15
IDENTIFYING OUR FEARS

"Courage is doing what you are afraid to do.
There can be no courage unless you are scared."

Eddie Rickenbacker

I promised you that this book would strive to be a useful tool. Not only would it allow you to learn about fears, but it would also assist you in two ways:

1. Identifying which of all the fears we've discussed affect you the most at this point in your entrepreneurship journey.

2. Preparing an action plan to overcome them.

So, fulfilling that promise, these last two chapters are your toolbox for effectively working on your fears. Like any toolbox, you can use it today for the fears that concern you now, but you can also keep it and use it later, at any other time, to work with new fears you encounter in different phases and stages of your journey as an entrepreneur. Remember that fears are dynamic. They come and go, change, grow, and diminish. At each moment in this entrepreneurial process, your fears will differ in type and intensity. So, I hope these last two chapters help you get to work.

Let's start in this chapter by helping you identify the fears you face at a given moment. I'll guide you to discover and reveal your fears.

Fear Disguises Itself

We don't always recognize fear as fear. It disguises itself as excuses. It searches for non-existent flaws to justify rejecting an opportunity. It seeks useless explanations that have nothing to do with the decision at hand.

Fear disguises itself because we don't like to accept it into our lives. We've been taught that being afraid is bad and that it's evidence of how cowardly we are, so we see it as something negative, something we don't want to be associated with in any way. Therefore, we give it a different name. We call it reasons or excuses for not doing something. We rationalize things to justify our reactions and behavior without admitting that we're afraid. It's not realistic to say we never feel fear about anything. Everyone has felt, continues to feel, and will feel some type of fear in the future. If we don't realize it, it's not because those fears don't exist or don't affect our decisions.

Since fear disguises itself and hides, it can be challenging to find and identify it. And if we don't find it, we can't overcome it.

Let's first understand the disguises that fear adopts. Here are some of the most common ones:

1. **Denial:** Denying or downplaying the existence of our fears is a common way to disguise them. We can convince ourselves that we're not really scared or that there's nothing to fear. Fear denial refers to the attitude of refusing or avoiding the presence or existence of fear within oneself. It's a way of psychologically shielding ourselves and avoiding fearful situations or emotions. Fear denial can be a natural response in some circumstances. However, consistently or chronically denying fear can be detrimental to emotional and psychological well-being. At some

point, we must acknowledge that we feel some fears. Otherwise, we'll never be able to overcome them.

2. **Avoidance:** Avoiding situations or circumstances that trigger fear is another way to disguise it. By avoiding confronting our fears directly, we can temporarily convince ourselves that they don't exist or aren't as significant since we're not facing them head-on. While this avoidance disguise strategy can provide immediate relief, it can be counterproductive in the long run. Constantly avoiding situations that trigger fear can limit our growth potential. It can lead to a negative cycle in which fear is reinforced and intensifies over time. By avoiding fearful situations, we miss the opportunity to learn that we can handle them appropriately and safely. This can lead to increased anxiety and decreased confidence in facing fears in the future.

3. **Rationalization:** Justifying or explaining our fears logically and rationally can be a way to disguise them. We may find logical or rational explanations or excuses for our concerns rather than acknowledging the underlying fear. When our fears are hidden behind logical reasons, we're not overcoming them. We accept that it's okay to feel fear and that there are reasons for it. That part is fine because it involves recognition. However, when we overexplain fear to the point of accepting it as an integral part of ourselves that cannot change, we're resigning ourselves to living with that fear. We're inviting it to share our lives. And that's not really in our best interest. Some fears are inherently irrational and cannot be addressed solely through logic. Additionally, attempting to rationalize a fear excessively can lead us to deny or minimize the legitimate emotions associated with it. Through this disguise, fear hides behind excuses. It's the famous "I can't because..." We try to rationalize the decisions we make based on fear to justify them without feeling guilty or acknowledging that we're afraid.

4. **Humor or sarcasm:** Using humor or sarcasm to cover up fears is common. We make jokes or sarcastic comments to distract ourselves or avoid delving into our true fears. Humor and sarcasm can act as a protective shield to disguise fear and prevent vulnerability from showing. When we turn to humor or sarcasm, we try to divert attention away from our internal fears, distracting ourselves and others. When someone uses this coping mechanism, they may make jokes or sarcastic comments about the fearful situation or even about themselves to relieve emotional tension. This strategy is effective in reducing stress and anxiety levels. However, it doesn't resolve our issue because we're not addressing it head-on.

5. **Boldness:** Sometimes, fear disguises itself or hides behind an exaggeratedly brave attitude. We act as if we're not afraid to avoid showing vulnerability to others or to maintain an image of strength, though this can have negative consequences. On the one hand, we're truly denying it (as in point 1), which prevents us from dealing with it properly. However, this doesn't mean it disappears. Additionally, pretending to be overly brave can make it difficult to access emotional support. If someone constantly appears strong and courageous, others may not recognize their need for help. Boldness can lead to emotional isolation and make it challenging to seek support when it's genuinely needed.

These disguises of fear contain it for a certain time. However, since they are not effective strategies for facing and overcoming it, they allow it to grow, accumulate, and later emerge more problematically. The disguise will eventually become too small, and it will no longer be effective.

Identifying and Understanding Our Fears

To properly identify the fears that affect our ability to undertake a successful venture, we must follow three steps:

1. Recognize that we have some fear.

2. Identify the causes of our fears.

3. Classify the fears we feel to address them properly.

Once we have completed these three steps, we can move on to finding solutions and devising a plan. This will be the subject of the next chapter.

The first step, recognition, is perhaps the most difficult. I will assume that if you have this book in your hands and have reached this point in its reading, it is because you have already accepted that you have fears and decided to work on them. If this is not the case, anything I tell you from this point forward will be irrelevant.

Begin by recognizing your fears. Accept that you have them. There is no shame in it; they are good because they keep you alert and prevent hasty decisions. Once you accept them and face them, thank them for their warnings, take them into account, if necessary, but don't cling to them. Let them go. Get rid of them. Send them away. Turn the page.

Next, I propose a set of exercises and dynamics that you can do in private, in the safety of your own privacy. Do not report to anyone what you find unless it is something you want to share with someone who can help you in this complex process. These exercises form a guided self-reflection exercise to help you identify your main fears. As you repeat it, it will become easier and easier to delineate them.

There is no pressure. There are no right or wrong answers. It's not a race. There's no rush. It's an exercise for you. Enjoy it and take advantage of it in a relaxed manner and at your own pace. After all, you are not accountable to anyone. No one is judging you. There is no grading or competition. So, you must be completely honest with yourself. It's not about seeking what you ideally want to feel. If you do the exercise expecting to feel good about the result or to show it off to someone, it loses its purpose. Be honest and transparent.

If you wish, you can download formats and support materials for these exercises at the following link, whether you want to do it by printing out the forms and working by hand or with digital records.

celiasoonets.com/the8fearsofentrepreneurs

Some tips before you start:

Find a quiet place without interruptions where you feel comfortable and at ease. It can be at home, at your workplace, in a park, at a café, at a family member's house, or in a garden—any peaceful and interruption-free place will do.

Set aside a couple of hours without breaks to work on the exercise. You can do them in stages, over several sessions, but try to have at least two hours for each session.

Take notes, write on paper, in notebooks, or digital format on a computer or tablet. Use the resource that is most comfortable for you, but make sure to write down your answers. Just thinking about the topics the exercise proposes is not enough. Until you write it down, you won't be truly immersed in the exercise with total commitment.

If you don't plan to use the downloadable formats and will work on paper with a pencil, have twenty blank individual cards on hand for use in the exercises.

The goal is to eliminate any pressure or distress. You must be comfortable and relaxed for the process to flow. The complete dynamics consists of six exercises:

1. Fear Storming
2. The Story of Your Fears
3. Discovering Disguised Fears
4. Enemies of Your Dreams
5. Find the Cause of Your Fears
6. The Ladder of Fear

Each exercise will take one to two hours. I suggest you set a plan and complete them consecutively. If possible, dedicate a day or a couple of days to this activity and do all six exercises in order at once.

If you don't have the time to do it that way, I suggest doing them on consecutive days. Dedicate at least one or two hours each day for six days to complete one exercise per day.

Exercise 1: Fear Storming

This exercise is equivalent to a brainstorming session, but this time, it will be a storm of fears. Unlike the brainstorming exercise, which is recommended to be done in a group, this is a self-reflection exercise for you. However, we will retain the general rules of brainstorming.

Production Phase

On a piece of paper, a blank document on your computer, a whiteboard, or wherever you prefer, start jotting down, without evaluating or overthinking, all the fears you feel right now in relation to your entrepreneurship.

It's crucial that you don't judge what you write. In fact, take note of everything that crosses your mind. You will have the opportunity to review it, discard the superfluous, organize it, and keep what you find useful.

Four rules:

1. Don't dwell too much on each idea. If it comes to your mind, write it down as it is. Don't seek perfection in wording or dwell on it too much.

2. Opt for quantity. Your goal is to produce a list containing the largest number of fears you feel threaten you. Write down the ones that seem significant to you, as well as the ones that appear insignificant.

3. Avoid criticism or prejudice during the idea production phase.

4. Accept any wild ideas that come to mind.

Organization and Selection Phase

Organize the fears you listed. To do this, write them down on another piece of paper, document, or sheet (depending on the medium you selected to work with), but write them based on some criterion of commonality. For example, you can group those related to financial reasons or those associated with the fear of not being prepared. Group them according to a criterion that you find suitable. You can create as many groups as you consider convenient.

Next, if possible, transform the fears in each group into one overarching fear. The idea is to simplify the list, eliminate repetition, and end up with a shorter list encompassing everything you produced in the first stage.

Then, select the five fears that affect you the most at this moment, the ones that have the greatest negative impact on your business. Write down those five fears on five individual cards, one on each card, and save them for later.

Exercise 2: The Story of Your Fears

This exercise aims to uncover persistent fears in your personal history—those that you have at this moment in relation to your entrepreneurship and those that have accompanied you, either buried or openly, throughout your personal and professional life.

Prepare a format with two columns. In the first column, list all the fears you have had in the past, whether they were recurrent and/or overcome, in relation to your entrepreneurship. Continue in the same column and add the fears you have recurrently experienced in your professional life, with previous jobs you may have had, bosses, colleagues, and clients.

Continue in the same column and add the fears you have recurrently experienced in your personal life, with your family and friends, and in social situations.

Once you have your complete list, in the column next to each fear, register whether you believe you have overcome it or occasionally experience it.

Select the five recurring fears you think have consistently affected you in some way throughout your history and that you have not yet overcome. Check if any of these fears are in the previous list. If you didn't include them among the top five in your fear storming, write them on new cards and place them with the previous ones. You can have a total of five new cards if all the fears you found in this exercise are different from the ones you found in the fear storming, or you may not have any additional cards if the five you found are the same as the five you selected in the previous exercise. Save the cards for later use.

Exercise 3: Discovering Disguised Fears

This exercise aims to discover if you identify with fears that may have never crossed your mind but that, once you become aware of them, you realize you indeed have them. Perhaps some of them are lurking or disguised, which is why you've never seen them, but by considering them, you may realize they are affecting you.

When I conducted the study on the fears of entrepreneurs, a common comment from those who filled out the questionnaire was that reading each of the items in the survey opened their eyes to the fact that they felt more fears than they had believed or imagined. The questionnaire consisted of eighty items, each representing a possible fear that an entrepreneur might face. In this exercise, I invite you to review that list to see if any of them are disguised and perhaps exist within you without you having noticed.

Read each item on the following list and place a mark next to those you currently feel.

Review the list of all those with a mark and select the five with the greatest negative impact on your entrepreneurship right now.

Once again, check if any of these fears are in the lists from the previous exercises. If you didn't select them from among the top five in your fear storm or the story of your fears, write them on new cards and place them with the previous ones. You can have a total of five new cards if all the fears you found in this exercise are different from the ones you found in the previous exercises, or you may not have any additional cards if the five you found now are among the same ones you had selected earlier. Save the cards for later use.

- Fear of making uncomfortable decisions
- Fear of losing family or social relationships I value because of my business
- Fear that the business will fail and I'll have to close it
- Fear that new competition will enter the market and push me out
- Fear that my family won't approve of my business idea
- Fear that products or services won't be delivered with the right quality
- Fear of facing uncomfortable moments
- Fear of making many mistakes in the products or services I deliver
- Fear that government policies will disadvantage my business
- Fear that the image of my business could be negatively affected
- Fear that equipment or machinery may get damaged
- Fear of having to take on tedious tasks
- Fear of encountering problems that affect my operation
- Fear that my family may doubt my ability to run my business

- Fear of disappointing my friends/acquaintances
- Fear of facing delays and unforeseen inconveniences
- Fear of not generating a stable income for my expenses and those of my family
- Fear of having to do things that I find difficult
- Fear of not knowing everything that's needed to run my business
- Fear of not generating sufficient profits
- Fear of feeling like I'm not achieving my goals
- Fear of not having the right judgment to make good decisions for my business
- Fear of new regulations or laws that may affect my business
- Fear of not being able to solve the problems that come my way
- Fear of looking in the mirror and seeing someone who didn't achieve their goals
- Fear that my friends/acquaintances might think it's a bad idea to start a business
- Fear of conflicts with colleagues or employees
- Fear that the country's economy is in bad shape and will affect my business
- Fear of having to start over if things go wrong
- Fear of not achieving the financial comfort I aspire to with my company
- Fear of customers asking me something I don't know
- Fear that my friends/acquaintances may think I'm incapable of succeeding
- Fear that my friends/acquaintances may think my business idea is bad
- Fear that systems won't work for me
- Fear of being exposed to lawsuits or legal problems
- Fear of feeling bad if things don't go well
- Fear of the possibility of new products or services emerging to compete with mine
- Fear of conflicts with customers

- Fear that my employees/colleagues will ask me something I don't know.
- Fear that the world economy is in bad shape and will affect my business.
- Fear that my professional image may be negatively affected.
- Fear of not having all the information I need to make good decisions.
- Fear of being emotionally affected if things don't go well.
- Fear of the possibility of new products or services emerging that compete with mine.
- Fear of getting into conflicts with customers.
- Fear of losing friends due to the business decisions I must make
- Fear that changes in my business sector may negatively affect me
- Fear of not being able to meet commitments on time
- Fear of having to demand things from my employees/colleagues that they won't like
- Fear of disappointing my family
- Fear of not being able to run my business successfully
- Fear of the business failing and being left with debts
- Fear that my competition has better products or services
- Fear of my personal image being negatively affected
- Fear that my competition is stronger than me
- Fear of being forced to do things I don't like doing
- Fear of the possibility of feeling like a failure
- Fear of not generating enough income to cover business expenses
- Fear that my employees will leave the company because they don't like working for me
- Fear of conflicts with my business partners
- Fear of spending my savings on my business and not seeing results
- Fear of not being able to pay my employees
- Fear of finding myself in situations where I don't know how to react

- Fear of losing the money I invest in my business.
- Fear of doing things that I find annoying.
- Fear of the possibility of going bankrupt.
- Fear that the demands of the business will exceed my capabilities.
- Fear of making a fool of myself.
- Fear that new taxes may be imposed in my industry.
- Fear that my colleagues/employees won't like the decisions I make.
- Fear of making mistakes or errors in the processes.
- Fear of experiencing unpleasant moments.
- Fear of becoming depressed if I fail.
- Fear of not knowing my business sector well enough.
- Fear of not being able to meet financial commitments with suppliers.
- Fear of wasting time and realizing I didn't achieve my goals
- Fear of thinking that my business may fail
- Fear of not having the necessary knowledge to make the right decisions
- Fear that my friends might think my entrepreneurial venture is absurd.
- Fear of having to step out of my comfort zone

Exercise 4: The Enemies of Your Dreams

This exercise aims to find the fears that could affect the future success of your entrepreneurship—fears that you might not realize you have but could hinder your path as an entrepreneur. This time, instead of starting with thinking about your fears, we'll start by thinking about your goals and objectives, the dreams of what you want to achieve with your business.

Once again, prepare a format with two columns. Label the first column "Dream" and the other "Fear that hinders it."

In the first column, list things you want to achieve with your entrepreneurship. These can be immediate or long-term plans. It's a list of your dreams related to your business.

Think about what is currently preventing you from reaching those dreams. In the second column, next to each goal, write down the fear you believe could limit your ability to achieve it. There, you'll have a new list of possible fears that burden you.

Review the list and select the five that have the most negative impact on your entrepreneurship right now.

Once again, check if any of these fears are in the lists from previous exercises. If you didn't select them among the top five in any exercise, write them down on new cards and place them with the previous ones. You can have a total of five new cards if all the fears you found in this exercise are different from what you found before, or you may not have any additional cards if the five you found now are the same as what you selected earlier. Save the cards for later use.

Exercise 5: Find the Cause of Your Fears

The specific objective of this exercise is for you to engage in self-reflection that helps you understand the reasons underlying each of the fears you have identified and listed. Remember that to overcome them, you need to understand them. It's not just about knowing what they are but understanding why they have decided to appear in your life and your entrepreneurship.

By now, you should have between five and twenty cards with fears. You'll have only five if you consistently obtained the same five fears in all the exercises, twenty if you got different fears in each exercise. You could have any number in between if you repeated some and not others in each exercise.

Work with each card individually. For each card containing a fear you elaborated on, try to reflect on the origin of that fear. What is it about that situation or event that you wrote on that card that scares you? Write it on the card, along with the fear itself.

Exercise 6: The Fear Ladder

This is the last exercise in this section on identification and recognition. This final part aims to prioritize those discovered fears and associate them with the eight fears of the conceptual model.

I'm providing brief descriptions of each of the eight fears that make up the conceptual model as a reference to refresh your memory and for you to use as an aid in this exercise:

1. **Fear of financial losses:** Fear of not generating enough income to cover business expenses, generate income for your family, and losing the resources invested.

2. **Fear of change in the rules of the game:** Fear of the appearance of taxes, laws, or regulations that negatively affect business. Fear of global issues in the national and worldwide economy.

3. **Fear of competition:** Fear that your competition is stronger, has better products and services, and will push you out of the market or harm your image.

4. **Fear of operational problems:** Fear of problems and conflicts with employees, partners, or your family and friends. Fear that inconveniences will prevent you from delivering quality products or services on time.

5. **Fear of feeling incapable:** Fear of not knowing enough about your business sector, not having the knowledge to make appropriate decisions, and facing uncomfortable situations due to your lack of knowledge.

6. **Fear of feeling like a failure:** Fear of realizing that you didn't achieve your goals, feeling like a failure, becoming depressed, and being emotionally affected. Fear of being unable to keep your business going and making good decisions.

7. **Fear of feeling uncomfortable:** Fear of making uncomfortable decisions, exposing yourself to unpleasant situations, being forced to do things you don't like or don't feel confident doing.

8. **Fear of being judged:** Fear that family and friends think it's a bad idea, disapprove of your business, think you're not capable of running it, or become disappointed in you.

Take all the individual cards you prepared and group them according to each of the eight fundamental fears. Think about and analyze which fundamental fear each one corresponds to, and place the ones related to the same fundamental fear together.

You may have many fears in some of them and very few or none in others. Note the number of specific fears you have associated with each fundamental fear.

List the eight fundamental fears in order, based on the number of specific fears you have assigned to them. Place at the top of the list the one with the most specific fears associated with it, then the second, and so on. The one at the bottom of the list will have the fewest specific fears associated with it.

> Which of the eight fears is at the top? That's the one you should tackle first.

If you've done this exercise thoroughly, it should have allowed you to identify the fears you face with your entrepreneurship and prioritize their importance and prevalence at this moment.

CHAPTER 16
OVERCOMING TODAY'S FEAR

"I have learned over the years that when one's mind is made up, this diminishes fear: knowing what must be done does away with fear."

Rosa Parks

Fear does not disappear. Nor should it disappear because it is positive. However, it is necessary to modulate and control it.

We have mentioned throughout this book that fear arises in the face of uncertainty—when we confront something that feels threatening, that we do not know well, and that we are not sure we can control. Conversely, when a threat presents itself that we know and understand how to handle, we feel less fear because we know we have control.

So, the primary resource for controlling our fears is to increase our awareness of our power. When we reduce uncertainty and increase control, we have less fear.

Knowing that we have the possibility to do something effectively leads us to do it. At the same time, taking that step boosts our confidence in our ability to control what causes us fear. As we act, we obtain favorable results, and these results reinforce our confidence in the possibility of control. Consequently, we learn not to feel fear in that situation or similar situations. Through the action that leads us to take control, we have reduced fear.

Let's say the process unfolds as follows (Figure 5):

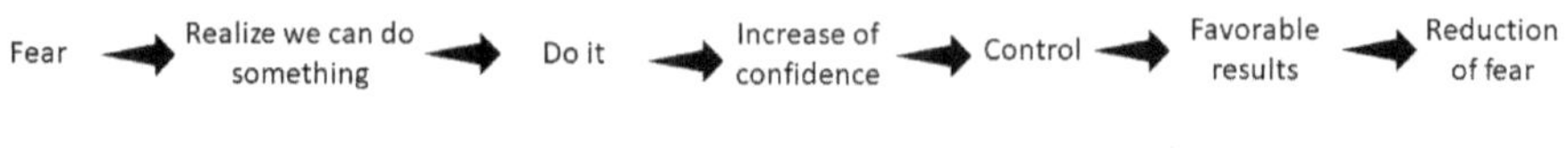

Figure 5 – Process of control of fear

This is a simplified way of seeing it, but the process works like this in each case.

Turning Fear into Drive

By acting in a planned and conscious manner in the face of your fears, you manage to turn your fears into motivation to act. The goal, then, is to convert your fears into motivations.

Fears are normal and inevitable. They are even welcome because they teach us to be cautious, but we must not let them paralyze us. From the moment we allow any of these fears we've seen throughout the book to prevent us from making relevant decisions, we have already begun to lose the battle. If we want to change fear, we must understand it for what it is—a sign of caution and prevention—and use it as a platform to move forward.

Don't feed fear. Do you remember in your childhood when any shadow on the wall looked like the most horrible monster? When the slightest noise convinced us that the ugliest bug had entered our room? This happened because we perceived the signs of unknown phenomena (noises, shadows), and our minds shaped them and made them grow. Unintentionally, we were feeding our fears.

The same happens with the fears we face in our entrepreneurship. If we feed them, we turn them into invincible monsters that paralyze us. But often, the enormous magnitude of these fears exists only in our minds, and by looking at them rationally, we can control and overcome them.

Developing Tolerance for Ambiguity

We have seen that one of the leading causes of our fears is uncertainty, ignorance about the outcomes we can expect from our decisions. Of course, the best way to resolve our fears is by reducing uncertainty. However, it is not possible to eliminate it completely. Therefore, to overcome our fears, it is important to learn to coexist with a certain level of uncertainty and ambiguity. How do we achieve this?

1. **Listening attitude:** The best tool for achieving openness to new experiences and the ability to understand what we do not know is to step out of our expert shell and humbly place ourselves in an intention to listen and learn from others and the new experiences we face. Curiosity, in this case, is a great virtue.

2. **Self-Criticism:** Recognizing our mistakes and weaknesses puts us in a better position to face new challenges. When we insist that our solution is the only or the right one or that we should do what we did in the past because "it worked before," we close ourselves off to the possibilities of discovering new, more efficient courses of action.

3. **Neutrality:** Avoid making judgments. The best way to learn and be open to new experiences is not to judge options before evaluating them. Judgments are generally based on our past

experiences and perceptions. And remember that, in this case, we are trying to open to a future we do not know or see clearly. Eliminate biases.

4. **Flexibility:** Be open to the possibility of change. Always be willing to adjust your course and try new things. The more flexible you are in your thinking and actions, and the more flexible your entrepreneurship is in its processes, the easier it will be for you to act with the agility required to overcome ambiguity.

5. **Proactivity:** Act toward the future, not the past. Anticipate your competition and market trends. Try to always stay one step ahead of others.

6. **Curiosity:** Curiosity serves as a catalyst for entrepreneurial success by fostering creative problem-solving, driving innovation, and promoting adaptability in the face of dynamic business challenges. Entrepreneurs with a curious mindset continuously seek to learn, adapt, and understand market trends, gaining valuable insights that contribute to informed decision-making. Overall, curiosity is a key driver that empowers entrepreneurs to stay ahead in the ever-evolving business landscape.

The Best Strategies to Overcome Entrepreneurial Fears

In each chapter, we have been discussing specific strategies to overcome each one. Here's a summary of them together. You will see that some are consistent for many of the fears, while others are more specific:

Fear of economic loss:
- Be better informed.
- Have a well-elaborated and detailed financial plan.

- Ensure pricing calculations include all costs.
- Understand your market.
- Seek support from professionals specialized in the field.
- Always consider a cushion to soften losses.
- Continuously monitor progress.
- Accept that some losses are inevitable.
- Understand seasonality in your business sector.

Fear of change in the rules of the game:
- Develop tolerance for ambiguity.
- Maintain an updated base of continuous information.
- Foster constant communication with customers, suppliers, and collaborators.
- Achieve flexibility in operations and strategies to easily adapt to market changes.
- Develop analytical thinking.

Fear of competition:
- Know and analyze your competition.
- Seek added value for your customers.
- Focus on your strengths.
- Focus on your niche.
- Seek differentiation.
- Strive for excellence.

Fear of operational problems:
- Maintain checklists and quality control.
- Regularly hold project status meetings.
- Prepare meeting minutes.
- Automate processes.
- Use agendas and task lists.
- Develop assertive communication.

Fear of feeling incapable:
- Carefully analyze the skills required for success and determine if you truly master them.
- Force yourself to accept compliments and recognition.
- Avoid perfectionism and accept that mistakes and failures are part of life.
- Avoid comparing yourself to others.
- List and celebrate your achievements.
- Identify and acknowledge the unique value in yourself and your entrepreneurship.
- Take more controlled risks.
- Develop more self-confidence.
- Cultivate self-compassion.

Fear of feeling like a failure:
- Plan with the appropriate rigor.
- Set intermediate goals that lead to the final goal and can be progressively achieved.
- Conduct scenario analysis and decision trees.
- Be prepared for the possibility of failure.
- Remove drama and negative connotations from failure.

Fear of feeling uncomfortable:
- Face your fears head-on.
- Develop self-confidence.
- Prepare for new experiences.
- Don't shy away from improvisation outside your comfort zone.
- Try doing things despite fear.

Fear of being judged:
- Know yourself.
- Work on your self-esteem and self-confidence.
- Trust your intuition and passion.
- Invest in yourself.

- Silence your internal critic.
- Accept that there will always be someone who criticizes you, no matter what you do.
- Prevent others' opinions from affecting you emotionally.
- Try not to let others' opinions guide your decisions.
- Stop judging others.

If we analyze the above list, which is detailed and explained in each chapter, we can see that some global, common strategies are expressed in a particular way but ultimately share the same foundation. Let's identify them:

1. **Planning, planning, planning:** I won't tire of giving you this advice. Adequate planning is the number one tool because more planning means less uncertainty, more control, and, consequently, less fear. Whether it's financial planning, operational planning, or marketing planning, it's essential to have it for the specific problem you're facing. But be careful; it's not enough to just have a plan. The plan is a living entity and a working tool. It's not a decoration to hang on the board to make you feel organized. Plans should be regularly reviewed. Quality control and monitoring mechanisms should be established to ensure that the plan is followed, and if it's not, adjustments should be made. Plans should change, progress, and adapt according to circumstances to achieve the objective. So: Plan and follow through with your planning.

2. **Seek all the information you need and a little more:** And formally analyze it. The best way to reduce uncertainty is to know what to expect or what might happen. So, whether it's understanding your market, knowing your competition, understanding the right technology, or understanding yourself, depending on the fear holding you back now, collecting, studying, and analyzing information is a fundamental tool. So: Investigate and analyze.

3. **Study and learn every day:** Continuous study and education are indispensable and intrinsic to entrepreneurship. Learning is an activity we should never (and don't want to) stop. Each new project, each new challenge, presents us with areas of knowledge we are unfamiliar with, and if we want to tackle them successfully, we must fill these gaps with new learning. You might say, "That applies to every professional, whether they are an entrepreneur or not." And that's true. Every professional, if they want to be successful in their field, must keep studying and updating constantly. What's different for entrepreneurs is that we must educate ourselves in more diverse fields, many even outside our area of specialization. This means that entrepreneurs must go through life with an eagerness for learning, a willingness to listen and discover. We must enjoy the educational process, actively seek it, and incorporate it into our daily routine. So: Study daily, never stop learning and preparing.

4. **Work on strengthening your self-confidence and self-esteem:** Know your strengths and weaknesses and capitalize on them. Learn to be proud of who you are and what you have achieved. Don't compare yourself to others or constantly seek validation and approval. When you have confidence in yourself and value yourself for who you are and what makes you unique, you learn to handle uncertainty better, find opportunities more easily, achieve your goals, become less vulnerable to others' opinions, and find alternative and creative solutions to your problems. All of this leads to an increased likelihood of success for your entrepreneurship. So: Love yourself and accept that you are strong and capable.

5. **Work on strengthening your self-compassion:** Cultivate a kind and understanding attitude toward yourself. Practice mindfulness. Recognize that you are a human being, subject to making mistakes and facing challenges. Treat yourself as you

would a friend in trouble or suffering. So: Be patient with yourself, forgive yourself, practice gratitude, and seek support if necessary.

6. **Take small and progressive steps:** To overcome any of the fears we've analyzed, it's not necessary to set the highest goal on the first try. That only makes it more difficult to dare. Break down the goal into smaller goals. Take controlled and small risks progressively. Each step forward will become an achievement that allows you to move in the right direction and, at the same time, becomes motivation and helps enrich your confidence and self-esteem. With each small achievement, you will feel less vulnerable and more in control. Consequently, you will gradually reduce your fear. So: Take small but constant steps.

7. **Seek help whenever necessary:** There is nothing wrong or shameful in asking for help when needed. No one expects us to be able to do everything and do it well. If you need a finance expert, a marketing expert, or a mentor to advise you, don't hesitate to seek them out. What you invest, in time and money, in specialized assistance pays off for your business by improving its competitiveness in the market and increasing its chances of success. So: Seek specialized advice if you need it.

> But above all, start by recognizing your fears and learn to accept them so that you can moderate and maneuver them. Only then can you overcome them.

Action Plan

Now that we have reached this point, I hope you have a clearer understanding of the fears that are weighing on you in relation to your entrepreneurship and that you have identified some strategies that can help you. Congratulations. But you're missing one last step. None of what we've learned here will be useful if we don't put it into practice, and guess what? It's time to plan.

1. Review your fear ladder that we created in the previous chapter.

2. Identify the fear that is impacting you the most right now.

3. Review the strategies for that fear in the table above and revisit the chapter. Reread it with a new perspective. Try to understand it better and think about actions you can take to overcome it.

4. Prepare a format with three columns. In the first column, write the title "Action," in the second column, write the title "Completion Date," and in the third column, write the title "Completed."

5. Write at the top the specific fear you want to control and overcome.

6. In the first column, write down three specific actions you plan to take to overcome it based on the strategy suggestions I've given you.

7. In the second column, put a specific date by which that action will be completed.

8. And most importantly: Regularly review the document to validate that you are doing what is necessary. Adjust if necessary and congratulate yourself once you can put a mark in the third column indicating that it is "Completed."

Repeat the exercises from these last two chapters every time you feel any fear on your path as an entrepreneur. Remember that fears will always arise. Welcome them. Listen to the alert they bring you. But do not allow fear to guide your decisions. Accept your fears, be thankful that you have them, and proceed immediately to design an action plan to overcome them.

Thank you for trusting me and this book. I hope these strategies help you now and in your future as an entrepreneur. I wish you a lot of success.

APPENDIX

Methodology for the Statistical Analysis of the

Global Study on Entrepreneurial Fears

March-May 2023

In this section, I will briefly present the methodology and analysis procedures used in the "Global Study on Entrepreneurial Fears" that I conducted between March and May 2023 to validate and refine the conceptual model proposed in this book.

The Questionnaire

Once I decided to delve into this topic beyond a blog article and started the project of writing this book, I realized that it was essential to validate the conceptual model with empirical data through research. Therefore, in March 2023, I began developing a questionnaire to conduct a study among entrepreneurs.

To create the questionnaire, I developed a battery of eighty items in total: ten items for each of the eight fears. This way, I had forty items related to fears of external events and another forty related to internal events.

Each item was expressed in terms of a statement in which the interviewee had to rate the frequency with which they experience that specific fear, using a four-point scale, as follows:

- Never
- Very rarely
- With some frequency
- Very frequently

Below are some examples of items:
- *Fear that the global economy is bad and will affect my business*
- *Fear of not being able to keep my business going*
- *Fear of getting depressed if I fail*
- *Fear of losing family or social relationships I value because of my business*
- *Fear that new competition will emerge and push me out of the market*

The specific question asked was: *"How often do you feel each of the following fears?"* For each of the eighty items, the interviewee had to decide whether they never feel that fear, feel it very rarely, feel it with some frequency, or feel it very frequently.

To avoid potential response biases caused by respondent fatigue as the response time progresses or by familiarity with the scale, I rotated the items extensively for each respondent. The items were presented in eight sets of ten, with the items related to all fears randomly mixed in each set. The eight sets appeared in a different random order for each respondent, and within each set, the order in which the items were presented also varied.

Additionally, I included some questions that allowed me to classify the respondents in terms of demographics (gender, age, level of education, country of residence) and in terms of their entrepreneurial activity (occupation, dedication to their entrepreneurship, time their entrepreneurship has been in the market, sector of entrepreneurship).

Data Collection

The fieldwork was conducted through a self-administered questionnaire available online, and a convenience sample was obtained. Although the questionnaire took only ten to twelve minutes to complete, the complete response rate was 64 percent. After two months, I closed the fieldwork in mid-May 2023, with a total sample of n=325 interviews, of which n=210 were completed. In the analysis process, I decided to eliminate four subjects whose responses indicated they "never" felt any of the eighty items of fear, leaving me with a final sample of n=206 individuals. Of these, n=138 were entrepreneurs with an ongoing business, and n=68 were individuals intending to start a business, with plans for future projects, or developing their business. I received responses from Spanish-speaking entrepreneurs from sixteen different countries.

It is important to clarify that this study is exploratory. It does not aim to be a representative sample of the Spanish-speaking entrepreneurial population. However, it allowed for the validation and refinement of the conceptual model. It is necessary and advisable to continue this line of study in subsequent research with larger samples, selected using criteria of statistical randomness and with item refinement based on the results of this initial exploratory study, and also expanded to other geographies

Data Analysis Procedures

For the data analysis, the following steps were taken:

1. Numeric values were assigned to the frequency rating scale of fear occurrence as follows: Never=0, Very rarely=1, With some frequency=2, Very frequently=3.

2. Two-factor analyses were performed, one with the forty items related to fears of external events and another with the forty items related to fears of internal events. In each case, a solution of four factors was requested, using the Principal Components method with Varimax rotation. The factors obtained explain 57 percent and 56 percent of the variance in the items related to external and internal events, respectively.

3. For each of the eight factors obtained in this exercise, the total points from the responses of each interviewee for each set of items that make up the factor were summed. This way, eight scores were obtained for each interviewee, one for each of the eight fears.

4. Although originally, ten items were developed for each fear, after the factor analysis, some ended up with only seven items, while others had ten or even fourteen. To eliminate biases due to the number of items in each factor, a new variable called "Fear Intensity" was created. This variable represents the relationship between the total points obtained by the subject in that specific factor and the maximum possible score for that factor (if the factor, for example, has nine items, the maximum score would be 3x9=27, in case the person indicated that they feel all nine of those fears "Very frequently"). Fear intensity is thus a value between 0 and 1, where 0 represents the absence of fear, and 1 represents maximum fear.

Each of the eight fears was analyzed based on this new "fear intensity" variable. The intensity was also calculated for the total of external fears, the total of internal fears, and the total of all eighty fears combined. This variable's intensity was then analyzed in the total sample and the demographic subgroups. For example, if we find that a particular fear has an intensity of 0.56 among, for instance, individuals under forty-five years old, it means that, on average, entrepreneurs in that age group feel 56 percent of the maximum possible fear for that specific fear.

5. A second analysis was performed with these data to establish the relative importance of each fear. This analysis aimed to identify the most frequent fears and their relationship with others. For this purpose, a ratio was calculated between the points obtained for that fear and all the points obtained for all fears. This way, the relative importance percentages of the eight fears were identified. Together, they sum up to 100 percent of all fears reported by the total sample, and the percentage of each fear indicates its relative importance compared to the other seven fears.

6. An attempt was made to identify homogeneous groups of interviewees based on this newly created variable called "fear intensity" to validate the existence of different types of entrepreneurs based on their fears. For this, a cluster analysis was performed using the k-means procedure, using only the eight intensity variables of each fear. Three distinct groups were obtained and analyzed separately.

Results

You can download an infographic document summarizing the main results at the following link:

celiasoonets.com\the8fearsofentrepreneurs

If you desire more information or details, please feel free to contact me by sending an email to celia@eslabonesdenegocio.com. I will gladly try to address any inquiries in this regard that have not been clarified with the previous explanations.

Acknowledgments

To **Gerardo Díaz,** who supported me in this project from day one to the last. His wise advice and suggestions, as well as the engaging discussions on the book's topics and the supporting research, greatly enriched the content and quality of this book. My first reader.

To **Andrea Díaz** and **Geradine Díaz,** who enthusiastically listened to me, supported me, and provided guidance with their opinions every time I needed to discuss the book's content or the adventure of publishing it. They also read it and gave me suggestions before the final version.

To **Paul Emond, Tim Redpath, Lara Quentrall-Thomas** and **Janelle Ifill,** who took the trouble of being the first readers and reviewing the initial draft of this English version with dedication and care.

To **Annette Levesque,** a fellow traveler in the publishing process with whom I shared many sessions of mutual learning.

To the entrepreneurs who selflessly responded to the survey, the results of which allowed me to validate the model presented in this book.

From the bottom of my heart, thank you.

References

Some of the books and documents that were part of the research process for the preparation of this book:

Albrecht, Karl (2015). *Inteligencia práctica.* B. De Books. Barcelona.

Barbabosa, Rafael; **Gomez** Esmeralda; **Daza**, Alexa; **Angeles**, Samuel (2021). *Psicología del miedo.* Boletín de la Universidad de Granada. Granada.

Bedoya Dorado, Cristian (2012). *El uso del miedo como herramienta de gestión y los efectos en los seres humanos y la organización.* Universidad del Valle. Santiago de Cali.

Budner, Stanley. (1962). *Intolerance of ambiguity as a personality variable. Journal of Personality,* 30 (1), 29–50. Connecticut.

Chaplin, J.P. (1968): *Dictionary of Psychology.* Third edition. 1985. Bantam Dell.

Delgado Reyes, Andrés Camilo; **Sánchez López**, Jessica Valeria (2019). *Miedos, fobias y sus tratamientos.* Revista Electrónica de Psicología Iztacala, 22 (2). Tlalnepantla.

Ekore, John; **Okekeocha**, Ogochukwu (2012). *Fear of Entrepreneurship among University Graduates: A Psychological Analysis.* International Journal of Management. Vol 29, Nº 2, Part 1. England.

Frenkel-Brunswick, Elsa (1949). *Tolerance toward ambiguity as a personality variable.* Journal of Personality, 18. Connecticut.

Gielnik, Michael; **Cardon**, Melissa; **Frese**, Michael (2021). *The Psychology of Entrepreneurship. New perspectives.* SIOP. Society for Industrial and Organizational Psychology. Routledge. New York.

Hawkins, David (2014). *Power Vs. Force.* Hay House Inc. Carlsbad, California.

Hayton, James; **Cacciotti**, Gabriella; **Giazitzoglu**, Andreas; **Mitchell**, Robert; **Ainge**, Chris (2013). *Understanding fear of failure in entrepreneurship: A cognitive process framework.* Enterprise Research Center. Boston.

Hemmi, Matti (2013). *¿Te atreves a soñar?: Ponle fecha de caducidad a tu sueño y sal de tu zona de confort.* Ediciones Paidós. Barcelona.

Jeffers, Susan (2007). *Aunque tenga miedo, hágalo igual.* Ediciones Robinbook. Barcelona.

Jericó, Pilar (2006). *NoMiedo en la empresa y en la vida.* Alienta Editorial. Barcelona.

Leary, M. R. (1983). *A Brief Version of the Fear of Negative Evaluation Scale.* Personality and Social Psychology Bulletin, 9(3), 371–375.

McClelland, David (1987). *Human Motivation.* Cambridge University Press. Cambridge.

Oros, Laura Beatriz (2005). *Locus de control: Evolución de su concepto y operacionalización*. Revista de Psicología de la Universidad de Chile. Vol. XIV, Nº 1. Santiago de Chile.

Plutchik, Robert (2003). *Emotions and Life: Perspectives from Psychology, Biology, and Evolution*. American Psychological Association. Portland.

Reyes-Sosa, Hiram y **Molina-Coloma**, Verónica (2018). *Análisis psicométrico de una escala para medir el miedo al delito en jóvenes ecuatorianos*. Universidad del País Vasco, San Sebastián, España. Acta. colomb.psicol. 21 (1): 290-299

Rotter, Julian (2017, Reprint of 1954). *Social Learning and Clinical Psychology*. Martino Fine Books. Connecticut.

Segura, J. A. (2019). *El emprendimiento y sus temores más frecuentes*. Universidad Militar Nueva Granada. Bogotá.

Vera-Martínez, Juan José (2020). *Las emociones del miedo, efectos en las organizaciones. Apuntes para las quejas en la comunidad universitaria*. Revista RUEDA, Nº 5. Murcia.

Vila, Jaime; **Guerra**, Pedro; **Muñoz**, Miguel, **Perakakis**, Pandelis; **Delgado**, Luis Carlos, **Figueroa**, Marlen; **Mohamed**, Sofia (2009). *La dinámica del miedo: la cascada defensiva*. Escritos de Psicología. Universidad de Granada. Granada.

About the Author

Celia Soonets holds degrees in Arts and Social Psychology from the Central University of Venezuela, with a Master's in Business Administration from UQAM (L'Université du Québec à Montréal).

Most of her professional career has been in the world of market research, marketing, and consulting. She began her career in the corporate world in 1987, where she held managerial positions for eight years.

Subsequently, she ventured into developing her own businesses, always in the field of market research, as a partner at Emevenca, a medium-to-large-sized company that began with offices in Venezuela and now provides services in the Dominican Republic, Jamaica, and Trinidad. She has over thirty years of experience in the market.

In 2006, she started a micro-business designing jewelry, Soonets Jewelry, which she worked on independently alongside her other ventures until 2019.

In 2019, she started a blog in Spanish for micro-entrepreneurs: Eslabones de Negocio (eslabonesdenegocio.com). Through this blog, she regularly shares topics related to values, attitudes, and habits that contribute to an entrepreneur's success and tools for achieving more efficient performance.

She has had experience within three different business environments: corporate as an employee, the private sector as a partner in a medium-to-large-sized company, and the private sector as a micro-entrepreneur in projects where she worked primarily alone. This has given her a broad perspective on the different aspects of the business world at each of these levels.

She is certified to administer and analyze the EMP (Entrepreneurial Mindset Profile), a tool from Eckerd College (Florida, USA), for assessing individuals' profiles across personality and performance dimensions related to entrepreneurship to help understand strengths and development opportunities for entrepreneurs.

With *The Wheel of the 8 Fears of Entrepreneurs*, her first book, she embarks on her journey as a writer.